HER

SAFE

RETIREMENT

HER SAFE RETIREMENT
Seven Strategies for Women to Retire Safely and Comfortably

ISBN: 978-1-956220-75-9

Expert
Press
www.ExpertPress.net

Editing by Elaina Robbins
Copyediting by Lucy Spencer
Proofreading by Geena Barret
Text design and composition by Emily Fritz
Cover design by Casey Fritz

HER
SEVEN STRATEGIES FOR WOMEN
SAFE
TO RETIRE SAFELY AND COMFORTABLY
RETIREMENT

ANDREW WINNETT

CONTENTS

INTRODUCTION

July 1, 2009, was just another Wednesday, as far as I was concerned. I was married and had a good job in the financial industry, where I was working on my normal opening procedures with my fellow bankers. My mom called and left a voicemail updating me on Dad's progress in trying to jerry-rig his "new" 1979 trailer in time for our Fourth of July camping trip. When she called a second time, I assumed she was updating me on the trailer situation and decided it could wait until break. Then I received another call right after the first one. That wasn't like her, so I excused myself to listen to that second voicemail.

As soon as I heard the sound of my mom crying, I knew something was wrong. I immediately called the house phone, and my fifteen-year-old sister picked up and, in between sobs, uttered the words I will never forget as long as I live.

"Dad's dead."

Instantly, I went into shock.

"What?" I cried. "How is Dad dead? What happened? Are you sure?" I'm not really sure what my sister said after my barrage of questions, but I assured her I was on my way. I left work and raced the normally twenty-minute drive from Roseville, California, to Auburn, where my parents lived. I remember all the memories racing through my head during those ten minutes of silence like it was yesterday: our last fishing trip two weeks earlier, for Father's Day, when I took him to my secret spot and "slayed" the trout; all the fights and reconciliations we had when I was growing up; all our camping adventures. Could he really be gone? I thought about my younger brother and sister still at home and about my future children who would never get to meet him, at least not in this life. A million thoughts and questions spun out of control.

When I finally blew through the last stop sign and pulled up to my childhood home, I was shocked to find multiple police and ambulance vehicles with lights on out front. I jumped over the planter row and plowed through the open front door to find a sheriff with his head down, avoiding eye contact. As I made my way to the open back door, the sound of my mom and sister crying greeted me before I stepped into the backyard.

Dad was lying on a stretcher, pale and unmoving. I stared at him for a long time in disbelief. Somehow, I didn't cry. I didn't break down for a while. The responsibility to be strong landed on my shoulders. It wasn't until later that the shock wore off and I lost it. My dad was gone.

In the days that followed, my family was left to pick up the pieces, trying to evaluate what to do next. My mom was mourning the loss of her best friend; we kids were mourning the loss of our dad. It was horrible. To make matters worse, my mom, a homemaker for twenty years, had no money. My dad had been accustomed to making six figures in the computer industry, but he had been laid off eighteen months earlier. They had been used to living on that $100,000 annually, and they had spent all their savings getting by while my dad looked for a new job.

By the grace of God, my mom had two term-life insurance products that were over a decade old. She received a little more than $400,000 in life insurance proceeds. It was definitely a lifesaver, but it wasn't enough to sustain the family indefinitely. My dad had been the primary breadwinner while my mom raised three kids, and he made enough money (and then some) until he lost his job. But now, what was my mom to do? The life insurance payout would last for four to six years of living expenses, depending on how much they tightened up their budget. Should she use the life insurance payouts for daily expenses with a $400,000 mortgage hanging over her head? Or should she pay the house off free and clear and have nothing to live on? My grandma ended up moving in to help make the house payments. It was a rough situation all around.

I see situations like my mother's almost every day. A lot of times, it's actually worse; at least my mom got something when my dad died. But even in her case, the concerns kept mounting. What about retirement? Would my mom have to go back to work while raising the kids? Would she have to go further into debt to go back to college? What would happen when my grandma passed away and the mortgage subsidy ended? What if my mom had to sell the house quickly and lose potential equity? And what if my mom got sick? Would she have to pay out of pocket and completely deplete any resources she had?

As the oldest, I felt totally responsible. I knew I needed to help my mother leverage her remaining funds to provide for herself in the long run. But how? What if I made a mistake? What if I lost some or all of her money? How could I help my mom retire with more than just her dignity?

Fast-forward to today. As I look back and write this book many years after my dad's death, I am blown away at how God uses all things for good, even really terrible things. You see, my dad died way too soon. But if he hadn't died, my mom and thousands of my company's clients would not have experienced the peace of mind of being *fully protected*.

My clients *know* they won't be leaving any financial burdens to their loved ones. Their next of kin won't have to push any humiliating crowdfunding websites begging for help. No bake sales. No car washes. No going bankrupt over a chronic illness or long-term care situation. No withdrawing a yearly 4 percent from whatever nest egg they managed to scrape together, hoping they don't outlive their money. No wondering whether it's better to die sooner rather than later because, frankly, they can't afford to live any longer. No counting on Social Security to be their main source of income. No more living in fear or asking "What if . . . ?"

In my mom's case, I had to go on a quest. I was already in the financial industry; I had planned to become a financial advisor—until I lived through the 2008 financial crisis while working at a well-known bank. When I saw our local financial advisor running around like a chicken with its head cut off trying to explain to his clients why their portfolio was down 40 percent, I realized I don't want to lose people's money—not one cent! It was all a setup for what was coming.

I'm pleased to say that today, my mom's "income silos" (including Social Security) pay her over $70,000 a year. (In this context, a silo is a bucket of money that's earmarked for either safety, income, growth, or estate planning. More on silos later.) That money will come in *every year*, no matter how long she lives. It doesn't matter if the market goes up 50 percent or down 50 percent. She will never have to go back to work or fulfill any college courses. She will never become another casualty of the healthcare system bleeding her dry. She has assets above the federal poverty line, and she won't have to deplete her resources before the government steps in and starts paying. She doesn't have to join the ever-increasing group of seniors filing for bankruptcy in their old age. Her long-term care is taken care despite a health condition she has.

My mom doesn't have to worry about her children getting the runaround when it's time for her to go to heaven and time for the remaining assets to be passed on. She is living the dream now. She is living life on her own terms, and she did it with the advice I'm going to share with you in these pages.

I hope my mom's story encourages you to see that even in the midst of a tragedy, if you follow the seven strategies in this book, you can do more than survive. This book is divided into seven chapters—one for each strategy. I didn't pick a holy number on purpose; it just happened to work out that way. I'll take it as a sign. Each of these strategies played a pivotal role in my mom's successful financial plan. In these pages, you'll learn about retirement income, risk reduction, tax savings, real estate investments, long-term care coverage, Social Security, and the one thing that holds most women back from financial freedom: fear. Using this information, you can change not only your own financial trajectory but also your family's trajectory for generations to come.

1
INCOME IS QUEEN

"How much have you saved for retirement?" Have you ever been asked that, or have you asked yourself that? It's a common question, not just among everyday women but among financial advisors as well.

On the surface, this question makes a lot of sense. Of course, financial advisors try to solve the problem of income in retirement by helping people save! Unfortunately, though, this approach is exactly the opposite of what I recommend. Starting with the question "How much have you saved?" is, in my opinion, an inferior approach with potentially dangerous consequences. Savings are commonplace; income is queen.

No, this doesn't mean you're stuck in the workforce forever. In fact, it means quite the opposite. In this chapter, I'm going to show you exactly how this approach works, starting with why the traditional retirement approach is one big scam perpetuated by the US government. I'm not a conspiracy theorist—once I lay out all the evidence, I'm sure you'll see where I'm coming from. Next, we'll cover how doing the opposite of what most financial advisors recommend can guarantee you an income that lasts as long as you do and leaves your heirs with a nice inheritance. Finally, I'll walk you through how you can work on building income no matter what stage of life you're currently in, from the workforce to retirement. Income is queen, and in this chapter, you'll learn how to reach into her pockets.

THE SINISTER 401(K) SCHEME

Let me tell you a little story about the sinister 401(k) scheme. This story actually starts with pensions.

Back in the day, companies created pension plans for a strange reason. During a chunk of the 1940s, it was illegal for companies to recruit workers from competitors by offering better pay.[1] Employers therefore had to get creative about how to attract talent to come work for their organization. That's where pensions came in.

Let's say you were working at Ford in the 1940s, and I was a manager at GM. I might approach you and say, "You're the cat's meow. You're super talented and knowledgeable. I know you're over at Ford, but I want you to come work for me at GM. I can't pay you more per hour

---

[1]   United States National War Labor Board, *Application of the "Little Steel Formula"* (Washington, DC: Division of Public Information, 1944).

than you're making now, but here's the deal: If you work for me for forty years and give me your career, I will give you 80 percent of your highest year's salary every year during your retirement."

As an employer, I seriously doubt you'll work for me for forty years; I'm more interested in the short-term benefits of hiring you. As an employee, however, you're thinking, "Where do I sign? This is a great deal! I just got my meal ticket. There are rivers of gravy ahead."

Fast-forward forty years into the 1980s, and all these people did indeed spend their careers at one company. Now it's time for those rivers of gravy. Retiring workers are holding their hands out, saying, "It's time to pay up, buddy." However, rising costs and the insane amounts of money companies had to shell out for these pension plans are unsustainable, and businesses are going bankrupt as a result.

My grandma happened to be one of the people who beat the system. She received a pension longer than she worked—retired in her mid-fifties, lived to 100 years old. She also received a pension from her husband with a 100 percent survivorship benefit for over forty-five years. She raked in two pensions for multiple decades, earning around $10,000 a month. It was insane, and she wasn't the only one who was able to do that.

THE BIRTH OF THE 401(k)

When all of these massive employers started struggling to pay large pensions, in stepped Ted Benna, the founder of the 401(k). He created a plan under the IRS tax code section 401, subsection (k), called a defined contribution plan. This new plan, commonly known as a 401(k) plan, allowed employers to incentivize talent in a way that wouldn't put them out of business.[2]

So, in the 1980s, if you're working at Ford and I'm at GM, my pitch now sounds a little different than it did forty years ago. I might say, "I want you to come work for me. I can't afford to give you a pension, but I will work with you on a 401(k) plan. You save a certain amount, and I will match it. We will work together to build this fund throughout your career. Then, when you're getting ready to retire, you can take that lump sum and buy a pension plan to fund your retirement." This was the entire purpose of the 401(k) plan: It was a backdoor way to get a pension.

The 401(k) was so successful that it led to the creation of other plans, including the 403(b), the 457, and the Thrift Savings Plan (TSP). Most people automatically sign up for these plans to this day; in fact, you probably have one yourself. However, you have probably never heard of buying a pension. What happened? I'll tell you what happened: Wall Street happened.

---

2   Ted Benna, *401k – Forty Years Later* (Maitland, Florida: Xulon, 2018).

"WHERE PURPOSE IS NOT KNOWN, ABUSE IS INEVITABLE"

Evangelist Myles Munroe authored one of my favorite quotes: "Where purpose is not known, abuse is inevitable."[3] In other words, if I take my four kids and go out on the weekends and start tossing them my phone like it's a frisbee, I'm abusing the purpose of my phone and am going to break it. The American middle class doesn't understand the purpose of the 401(k), which is why it tolerates Wall Street abusing these accounts every single day.

In the 1980s, as retirement savings plans gained in popularity, Wall Street saw trillions of dollars pouring into these accounts. They started rubbing their hands and licking their chops, saying, "Oh, baby, how do we get access to all that money? How can we convince the American middle class not to put their money in a pension where it's safe? They should give it to us so we can put it in the market, lose it, and charge a massive fee for our services!" And that's exactly what happened.

According to a Nerdwallet.com survey, the average American pays $1.1 million in fees over their lifetime.[4] Think of it: Every person represents $1.1 *million* in fees

---

3   Myles Munroe, *Rediscovering the Kingdom: Ancient Hope for Our 21st Century World* (Shippensburg, PA: Destiny Image, 2004), 116.

4   Erin El Issa, "Financial Fees Could Cost Americans $1.1 Million Over Their Lifetime," NerdWallet, updated August 7, 2018, https://www.nerdwallet.com/article/investing/financial-fees-study-2018.

over their lifetime. No wonder Wall Street is buying up all these media companies and force-feeding us this narrative about keeping money in the market! When you're in your twenties, thirties, forties, or fifties, that's fine and even beneficial. You can have money in the market because those are your accumulation years. The market goes up, the market goes down, and you have time to recover and recuperate, thanks to your paycheck. But when you get toward the top of that retirement mountain and start your descent, it's no longer sustainable.

It's no wonder that, according to a recent National Bureau of Economic Research study, almost one out of every two people in America runs out of money before they run out of life. I'll say it again: *Almost one out of every two Americans runs out of money before they run out of life.*[5] What the heck is going on? We have a 50 percent failure rate. I don't want the success or failure of my retirement left up to a coin flip. Heads, I don't run out of money; tails, I die broke. That's not the way that I want to retire. What about you?

---

5   James M. Poterba, Steven F. Venti, and David A. Wise, "Were They Prepared for Retirement? Financial Status at Advanced Ages in the HRS and AHEAD Cohorts," National Bureau of Economic Research, (February 2012), https://doi.org/10.3386/w17824.

DON'T RELY ON SOCIAL SECURITY

If you're thinking, "That's awful, but at least I have Social Security to help cushion that blow," don't count on it. I am one of the producers of the Hollywood documentary *The Baby Boomer Dilemma*. (If you go to our website, www. retirementrenegade.com, we can send you a free copy.) We got all kinds of experts involved—Nobel-winning economists, state comptrollers, PhD experts, the whistleblower of the largest financial fraud in American history, the foremost expert on inflation. We even got the founder of the 401(k) on board. We did not pay any of them a penny to star in this film, nor did we tell them what to say. They didn't have an ax to grind, a dog in the fight, an agenda, or a bias. They were simply trying to warn the baby boomers about what's coming in the next ten to fifteen years.

In the movie, Olivia Mitchell, the foremost Social Security expert in the world, discusses how Social Security will be out of money by 2034 (as of the writing of this book, the date has been moved to 2033) and will have to reduce its benefits by a third across the board. Note that Social Security is not just an American thing; other countries have their own versions. They just don't call it Social Security.

The crux of the move is that Social Security is a giant Ponzi scheme. Yes, you read that correctly: It is a *giant Ponzi scheme*. When I save money and pay my Social

Security tax, that does not go into an account reserved for me. Instead, when I'm ready to retire down the road, that money that I've saved my entire life is gone. My Social Security taxes pay for someone's Social Security benefits today. My taxes pay their benefit, not my own. At some point, the whole house of cards will come crashing down. That's exactly what a Ponzi scheme is. *Bernie Madoff ran one of the biggest Ponzi schemes and was sentenced to 150 years in prison. Politicians create and run a Ponzi scheme to fund Social Security and get re-elected! It's disgusting!*

Today, we have a swelling elderly population and we don't have enough taxpayers to cover the rising costs of Social Security, Social Security Disability, Medicare, and Medicaid. That's why the government will have to reduce benefits across the board by 2033. Unless we extend the full retirement age, which is widely unpopular, or raise taxes by a *ton*, which is also widely unpopular, we will run out of money.

We filmed the movie in 2021, but since then, the estimated time frame has accelerated. Initially, the members of the Social Security Board of Trustees projected that Social Security would run out of money and have to reduce its benefits by a third in 2040. They then revised the projection to 2035, followed by 2034, and now it's 2033.[6]

---

6   Scott Horsley, "Social Security Is Now Expected to Run Short of Cash by 2033," NPR, March 31, 2023, https://www.npr.org/2023/03/31/1167378958/social-security-medicare-entitlement-programs-budget.

It's possible that we might see the one-third reduction occur even sooner unless legislators extend the full retirement age by approximately two years, raise Social Security taxes, and lower cost-of-living adjustments. Implementing all of these three changes would essentially help improve the financial stability of the Social Security system. However, it would be a significant setback for both current and future recipients of Social Security. But at the end of the day, Social Security is underfunded; we just don't have enough money. While it's possible that this time frame could be moved up further, this is a critical consideration in the retirement puzzle.

So your 401(k) is based on a lie, and your Social Security payouts are unreliable. What can you do? Simply save up? I hate to tell you this, but that doesn't work either.

LUMP SUMS VERSUS INCOME

Like I mentioned during the introduction, a lot of people try to plan for retirement by simply saving up a lump sum. This is because they believe they can live off the same withdrawal rate, using the growth of their portfolio as income. Traditional financial advisors usually say that if you save a certain amount and stick to the 4 percent safe withdrawal rate, you'll never run out of money. This used to be a million dollars but has increased over time—nowadays, it's anywhere from $1.5 million to $3 million. Either way, the idea is that if you are a certain age and spend a certain amount per month, having a specific amount saved up will prevent you from running out of money.

Unfortunately, that is not necessarily accurate. This system is vague, obscure, and ambiguous, with a lot of room for error. First, inflation used to be around 2 percent, but now it's a lot higher. Second, people are living longer, so they need more money. Dr. Wade Pfau, from the American College of Financial Planning, has stated that in the case of a married sixty-five-year-old couple, there is a 50 percent chance that one of those spouses will live to age ninety-six.[7] That's a long time to be retired! Third, long-term care costs are the number one cause of bankruptcy in America. Will your safe withdrawal rate cover that?

That's not even an exhaustive list. What if Social Security gets cut by a third sooner rather than later? What if a spouse dies prematurely? What about global instability, an economic crisis, a war, or another pandemic? The point is that financial advisors will choose a lump sum number and assume that none of these other factors will inhibit your safe withdrawal rate. That's just not smart.

---

7   Wade Pfau, "How Long Can Retirees Expect to Live Once They Hit 65?," *Forbes*, August 25, 2016, https://www.forbes.com/sites/wadepfau/2016/08/25/how-long-can-retirees-expect-to-live-once-they-hit-65/?sh=44f5b94d6b4f.

To make matters worse, the 4 percent withdrawal rate is drastically too high. In the current market, with stocks and bonds performing less reliably, economist Dr. Wade Phau says the safe withdrawal rate is around 2.8 percent.[8] So, even if you save a million dollars and use the 4 percent withdrawal rate, you can still run out of money prematurely. Thus, if you have a million dollars, you can only draw $28,000 per year. Is that enough for you to comfortably retire on?

The lump sum approach is based on several flawed assumptions. First, you don't quite know exactly how much you need to save. Second, your safe withdrawal rate is a lot lower than they're telling you. Third, you don't know how long your money will need to last because you don't know how long you'll live. (Most people who live to be 100 years old didn't believe they'd last that long.) So financial advisors are basing your entire retirement model upon three faulty premises.

So far, this chapter has been a lot of bad news. The good news is that things are looking up from here on out. We just have to flip our approach and focus on the queen.

---

8   Benjamin Felix, "EPISODE 89: Wade PFAU: Safety-First: A Sensible Approach to Retirement Income Planning — Rational Reminder," *Rational Reminder*, October 26, 2021, https://rationalreminder.ca/podcast/89.

THE BLESSING OF PREDICTABLE INCOME

Everyone wants retirement bliss, and the key to achieving this is through a safe and secure income that comes in every month regardless of market fluctuations, socioeconomic situations, political power, war, or bear markets. We want something we can count on. The goal is not about having a certain amount saved in retirement—it is about having a steady stream of income you cannot outlive. That's what a pension provides, and that's what a 401(k) is supposed to provide.

One 2012 survey queried many different Europeans to try to determine the common denominator of happiness.[9] The interviews revealed that people with a steady stream of income they can outlive, such as pensioners, are the happiest group. Conversely, those who don't have a steady stream of income they can outlive are the saddest, most disgruntled group of people in all of Europe.

These people were also most likely to encounter chronic illness due to fear or stress, which is the number one cause of premature death. Stress, a silent killer, is directly associated with the six leading medical causes

---

9   Irena E. Kotowska, et al., "Second European Quality of Life Survey: Family Life and Work," European Commission, 2010, reprinted in Ideas, *Time* online, May 2012, https://ideas.time.com/wp-content/uploads/sites/5/2012/02/ef1002en.pdf.

of death.[10] Yes, not having your financial affairs in order leads to massive amounts of cortisol spikes and serotonin, which can lead to premature chronic illness and ultimately premature death!

So, for your well-being, longevity, and happiness, prioritize income. Rather than trying to save a lump sum to avoid running out of money, you should come up with a monthly income that covers all of your bills plus fun money and hobbies. Do this by asking yourself, "How much do I need to live on today?" Not tomorrow, not ten years from now, but right now. This includes everything from fun money, gifts, and travel to bills, loans, taxes, and more. Once you know that amount, set up your finances so you have that amount coming in each month during retirement. That is really the key. It is not necessarily about how much you have saved; that can fluctuate depending on the market. Instead, it's about how much income you can *count* on.

You have to remember to factor inflation into this amount. If you set yourself up with an income of $10,000 a month to match your expenses, but that amount never increases, you would be in trouble. In five years, $10,000 won't be enough to meet the same needs it currently meets. You'll likely need around $12,000 or $13,000, depending

---

10   Michelle Pugle, "Can Stress Cause Death?," Psych Central, updated on June 30, 2022, https://psychcentral.com/stress/is-stress-the-number-one-killer.

on inflation. Therefore, your income must increase with time.

Think about it: If you have a $15,000 monthly pension coming in, your bills are $10,000, and your income will go up to account for inflation, it doesn't really matter how much you have saved. You could have a hundred grand or a million dollars saved for retirement, but that won't necessarily matter because you have your income coming in—a steady stream of income that exceeds your expenses and that will keep coming in for as long as you need it.

Once you have addressed the required monthly income, everything else becomes an added bonus. You can focus on growth, real estate, estate planning, and other areas. After securing the necessary income, once that income silo is taken care of, then everything else becomes more manageable. You can enjoy greater security, peace, and happiness during retirement. Doesn't that sound nice?

That is what I help people do—I help people obtain this income. That's what it's all about. If your bills are $10,000 per month, what if there was a way for you to have $12,000 coming in every month that grows to offset inflation? That would provide a tremendous amount of peace of mind compared to a static lump sum, wouldn't it? That's the point, and that's what I want to help you achieve.

THE SOCIAL SECURITY STOPGAP FUND

The income-based approach to retirement has to account for the instability of Social Security as well. You don't want a one-third reduction in your standard of living when Social Security is cut. I highly recommend creating what I call a Social Security Stopgap Fund to prevent this; it's what I do for my clients. When setting up your income, take a pool of money and put it in a product like a guaranteed increasing income annuity with a guaranteed growth rate. This fund will grow continuously; if and when Social Security is cut, you can turn on the Social Security Stopgap Fund to offset the difference. In certain situations, you may even end up making *more* than you would have made without the fund.

If you have a financial advisor and they haven't discussed this option with you, they either don't know about it or they don't know how to solve the problem. You should get a second opinion because this is a significant issue.

THE SILO STRATEGY

Bringing in a stable income during retirement may sound wonderful but far-fetched. That's why I wrote an entire book on the Silo Strategy called *Retire Without Fear* (formerly *The Joseph Strategy*).

Retire Without Fear is a guide on how to famine-proof your retirement using a famine-proof Silo Strategy. The strategy basically emulates what the biblical figure Joseph did to save not just Egypt but the entire known world during the worst famine in recorded history.

I believe Joseph in the Bible was the greatest financial advisor to ever live. I built my entire firm off the five principles that book is composed of. If you'd like to get a copy of it, you can go to www.retirementrenegade.com and request a free copy. However, I've included a distilled version of the information in the book here.

In farming, a silo is a large, tall, metal cylinder that is filled with grain to get farmers through leaner times. In retirement planning, a silo is a bucket of money that's earmarked either for safety (emergency fund), income, growth, or estate planning (long-term care and death benefit). The Silo Strategy is basically a combination of four well-stocked silos.

THE SILO STRATEGY

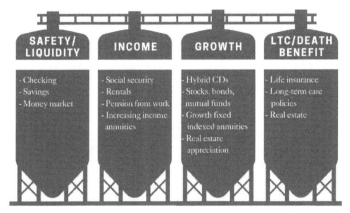

SAFETY/ LIQUIDITY	INCOME	GROWTH	LTC/DEATH BENEFIT
- Checking - Savings - Money market	- Social security - Rentals - Pension from work - Increasing income annuities	- Hybrid CDs - Stocks, bonds, mutual funds - Growth fixed indexed annuities - Real estate appreciation	- Life insurance - Long-term care policies - Real estate

LTC (Loan to Cost)
CDs (Certificate of Deposit)

THE SILO STRATEGY

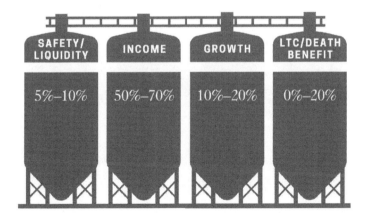

SAFETY/ LIQUIDITY	INCOME	GROWTH	LTC/DEATH BENEFIT
5%–10%	50%–70%	10%–20%	0%–20%

These financial silos are shown in order of importance, on a scale of one to four. From left to right, we have a safety or emergency fund, an income fund, a growth fund, and an estate planning or death benefit fund. I'll go over each of these silos in detail, as each one has a different purpose. Each category has a general percentage of your overall net worth allocated to it. For instance, if you have a million dollars, you will usually allocate 5 to 10 percent to the safety or emergency fund. The percentages I recommend in this section are generalizations and may vary based on individual needs, desires, concerns, and level of savings.

1. EMERGENCY FUND

Safety or liquid emergency funds form the most important silo. You have to have cash in the bank for unforeseen circumstances. You may suddenly need a new car. Fluffy may get sick and land you with a $10,000 vet bill. Your roof may get blown away, or your HVAC unit might explode. This fund is meant for situations like these.

Your emergency silo usually contains $50,000 or so; you may need a little more or less, depending on your situation. This safety or liquidity fund is designed so that it is accessible in a pinch. It is designed to give you access when needed. However, it won't see much growth.

2. INCOME

The second most important factor, after safety, is income. Your income needs to cover potentially thirty to forty years of retirement. Fifty to seventy percent of your retirement savings, which typically equals $500,000 to $700,000 (depending on monthly expenditures, including fun money and travel), should be allocated to income.

Once you have established your emergency fund and you have saved around $50,000 to $70,000 for it, you need to *really* address the income issue. This is where the Silo Strategy comes into play. I'll get into detail about that in the following section.

3. GROWTH

Once your income is secured, you can focus on growth. It is the third most important thing. Anywhere from 10 to 20 percent of your savings could be allocated to growth. Usually, this includes short-term and long-term growth.

Growth is typically intended for future expenses, such as a big trip down the road, saving for a new car, college planning for a child or grandchild, or even a new lake house. It is just designed to grow, and if it is not consumed during your lifetime, then ultimately it will be left behind.

4. ESTATE PLANNING

Fourth, we need to address long-term care or death benefits. Anywhere from 10 to 20 percent should be allocated to this category. Of the four silos, this is the least important, but it's still necessary.

Why is this the least important? Let's say you have the Cadillac of long-term care plans—you got it really dialed in, but you didn't take care of the second category, which is income. If you can't pay for the grocery bill when you're in your eighties, who cares about your cool Cadillac long-term care plan? You can't pay your bills! Therefore, it is essential to prioritize income.

INVESTMENT VEHICLES FOR THE FOUR SILOS

The Silo Strategy basically ensures that if famine hits, your income is guaranteed and secure within safe institutions. This means that when you're constructing your financial silos, you can invest in growth products that might be higher risk but have greater upside potential. Even if your growth silo fails or you lose a significant portion of it during a market decline, your planned income continues to come in. Your essential monthly bills, taxes, and discretionary spending are covered no matter what. You are financially secure, no matter what happens.

FUNDING YOUR INCOME SILO

Your income silo can include annuities, a pension, Social Security, or real estate income. Having income from different sources is wonderful, and the more you have, the better. However, if you don't have real estate income or a pension from work, the best way to solve your income needs is through an increasing income fixed index annuity.

Our firm prefers to use increasing income annuities to solve the income silo. There are so many reasons for this.

- They are the most guaranteed sources of income.
- You can't lose money in the market with increasing income annuities.
- There are liquidity options if you need access to your funds.
- Often, there is an up-front bonus to offset any investment losses in your IRAs or 401(k)s.
- They can provide long-term care benefits.

Let's say your income number right now is $40,000 annually. If you subscribe to the old method of saving a million dollars and collecting a 4 percent withdrawal rate (remember, this is actually too high—a 2.8 percent safe withdrawal rate is more realistic), you can get that annual $40,000 from your different investment accounts as long as you have a million dollars invested. But did you know that you can get that same $40,000 payout with only a $600,000 investment using fixed index annuities? And this can grow, lasting you the rest of your life, regardless of the market's performance? A million dollars with a 4 percent withdrawal rate achieves the same result, but using fixed income annuities, you need $400,000 less to *still* earn the same amount each year.

THE SILO STRATEGY BY AGE

No matter where you are in your life—whether you're building your career, a few years out from retirement, or actually retired—there are steps you can take to build your silos. Here's what I would recommend for women at various stages of their retirement journeys.

A quick note: If you're in your first half-century of life, you have a unique opportunity to start planning now. First, if your employer offers a match program, utilize the match up to the amount they're matching. Many of the other suggestions I have for you are too broad to discuss here, but you'll see them as they come up later in this book.

THE RETIREMENT RED ZONE

In the movie *The Baby Boomer Dilemma*, Ted Benna, the founder of the 401(k), talks about the retirement red zone—the five years before and after retirement. He said, "If you are in the retirement red zone and you lose 20 percent of your money in the stock market, you'll never recover it." Now that is shocking and very scary.

What does this mean for you if you're in that red zone? Well, if you're five years away from retirement, now might be the time to start taking some of your winnings off the poker table. You're up, so cash out while you're ahead and put some of that money in safer, less risky investments. If you lose 20 percent, which happens once every three and a half years (according to stock market statistics, that's how often we have a bear market),[11] then you may never see that money again. And that's terrifying.

You don't want to have to defer retirement because you happened to retire into a bear market instead of a bull market. If you retire into a bull market, everything's fine—it doesn't matter what you invest in. But you don't know what you'll retire into. It's a fifty-fifty chance, and I don't like those odds. Most people don't. So don't procrastinate and say, "I'll deal with this when I get closer to retirement." Talk to your advisor and figure it out. If you need help, feel free to reach out to our team.

The same applies after you retire. The last thing you want to do is lose 20 to 30 percent of your retirement

11   "10 Things You Should Know about Bear Markets," Hartford Funds, accessed April 20, 2023, https://www.hartfordfunds.com/practice-management/client-conversations/managing-volatility/bear-markets.html.

savings, then suffer through a flat market for a few years when you need that money to live on. Then, you have to go back to work because you took a 20 to 30 percent hit and your portfolio can't support you.

So, what should you do five years before retirement? You need to get a *less* risky strategy. Get your Silo Strategy in order, and make sure your income silo (50 to 70 percent of your overall portfolio) is really designed for income. It has to be safe; it can't decrease—no matter what happens. This will ensure you can still retire on time. Once you do retire, your Silo Strategy goes to risk tolerance, which we will discuss in the next chapter.

INCOME FOR LIFE

I hope I've convinced you that traditional retirement isn't good enough for you to gamble your future on. Lump-sum retirement strategies with fixed-rate withdrawals don't take into account factors like inflation and modern longevity. The 401(k) system is rigged, and Social Security is a Ponzi scheme. That's why my recommendation is to do the exact opposite of what most financial advisors advise you to do, and make Joseph your example.

Financial advisors suggest collecting a certain amount in savings, withdrawing a percentage of it each year, and living on that fixed amount regardless of your actual needs. If you do it the opposite way—calculate your monthly budget, then figure out how you can earn what you need every month—you can invest 40 percent less than you would have invested otherwise! Additionally, you're guaranteed to never lose any money, making it a much better way to solve the income problem.

Rather than coming up with a lump-sum number using an inflated safe withdrawal rate, create an income plan based on your actual monthly needs. Ask yourself or your financial advisor questions like, "What do I need to do to guarantee that my monthly amount is coming in every single month? How do I make sure my income is increasing each year to help offset inflation?" Figure out how to guarantee that your income will continue to be there for the rest of your life regardless of how long you or your spouse lives. If you're still building your career, only contribute up to the match of your employer, and invest as much as you can in tax-free or after-tax accounts to pay less in taxes over the long run.

If you're feeling overwhelmed by this, don't worry. We offer a free fifteen-minute phone consultation to get your specific questions answered. You can simply go to www.retirementrenegade.com to request your free, no-obligation consultation so you can know how to set up your retirement for guaranteed success!

2
RID YOURSELF OF RISK

Can you *really* remember how you earned your money? If you're nearing retirement, think back over the last twenty to forty years. Think of all the effort, the time, the energy, the difficulty. All the skills that you had to learn, the obstacles you had to overcome to get to where you're at today. Really *think* about all the energy you expended to acquire your money. Whether it's half a million, one million, or three million dollars, that dollar amount represents twenty, thirty, or forty years of your life's efforts and energies. It is the culmination of your hard work and dedication.

Here's why it's so important to remember this. If your financial advisor makes a mistake and puts that money in a super high-risk portfolio that decreases by 30 percent during a market crash when you need it most, they may have just lost ten years of your life's efforts, energy, and expenditure. It's brutal, but you have to view it in this manner. Waking up one morning to check your portfolio and realizing you've lost that much is devastating, especially as you approach retirement.

In the beginning of your career, risk is okay. You have time to bounce back if something happens. But as you get closer to retirement, risk is no longer acceptable. You don't have as much time to recuperate. So, in this chapter, we're going to examine this crucial topic: risk. You'll learn why and how people run out of money so fast, and you'll discover the power of low-risk investment options. By the end of this chapter, you'll be equipped with the knowledge to navigate the risks, find your risk tolerance, and explore investments that will actually see you through retirement. But, before we do all that, let's talk about the highest peak in the world.

THE MOUNT EVEREST TRAJECTORY OF SAVINGS

Did you know that more people die while descending Mount Everest than while ascending it?[12] When I first learned this, I didn't understand why this was the case. But when you really think about it, it kind of makes sense. When you're climbing up the mountain, you're focused, energized, and determined to reach the top. You eat your

---

12   Jordan Lite, "Death on Mount Everest: The Perils of the Descent," Scientific American Blog Network, December 10, 2008, https:// blogs.scientificamerican.com/news-blog/death-on-mount-everest-the-perils-o-2008-12-10/.

Wheaties every morning, and you have your eye on the prize. You're motivated to make it to the summit and victoriously plant your flag.

This is where mistakes happen. People often stay up at the top too long, get altitude sickness, and become fatigued and disoriented. Then they just want to go back down and climb into their sleeping bag down at base camp. People make the wrong choices, overdo it, go too fast, and end up losing their lives. It's macabre, but you can visit Mount Everest today and see the frozen remains of people who passed away hundreds of years ago. They're still up there to this day.

Those folks may have fared better if they had hired a Sherpa. A Sherpa is a special type of Himalayan guide who helps climbers reach the summit. They're used to carrying heavy loads of gear, setting up camps, and providing guidance throughout the journey. These experts possess exceptional mountaineering skills and know the terrain like the back of their hand.

Part of the reason Sherpas are so helpful is because they have different strategies and goals when ascending and descending the mountain. They know going up is very different from going down. When climbing up, they are all about supporting and guiding the climbers to make sure they have a safe and successful ascent. But once the climbers have reached the summit and start making their way down, the Sherpas' priorities change directions too. Sherpas are hyper-vigilant during the descent, constantly monitoring their clients and scanning the terrain for hazards.[13]

TWO DIRECTIONS, TWO SHERPAS

Now it may sound dramatic, but retirement planning can be a lot like scaling Mount Everest. The ascent represents your years of accumulating wealth, which span from your twenties to early sixties. During this time, you work hard and save money for your future. It doesn't matter if the market goes down, since you have time to recover, and you have a paycheck you can count on to meet your immediate financial needs.

However, as you approach retirement, you enter the decumulation phase, or the beginning of your descent from the mountain. Once you're descending, the Sherpa

---

13   Peter Zuckerman and Amanda Padoan, *Buried in the Sky: The Extraordinary Story of the Sherpa Climbers on K2's Deadliest Day* (New York: W.W. Norton, 2012), 25.

strategy, or the retirement strategy that helped you reach the summit, is no longer applicable. This is extremely important, so I'll say it again: *The retirement strategy that helped you reach the summit may not necessarily be the best one to ensure a safe descent.*

In finances, why is this? It's because, just like on Mount Everest, going down the mountain takes different priorities and a unique skill set. And while one Himalayan Sherpa may be able to handle both going up and coming down Mount Everest, in the financial world, you often need a different "Sherpa" to make your way down. This is because 99 percent of financial advisors focus on wealth accumulation. That's good and necessary when you're going up the money mountain, but overly risky wealth accumulation often results in retirement plan failure before people pass away. Yes, that's actually true, according to a variety of reports, including one report from the Center for Retirement Research at Boston College. That one found that the percentage of American households at risk of running out of money in retirement increased from 31 percent in 1989 to 50 percent in 2016.[14]

The growth accumulation model preferred by nearly all financial advisors is good, but incomplete. These

---

14   Alicia H. Munnell, Wenliang Hou, and Geoffrey T. Sanzenbacher, *National Retirement Risk Index Shows Modest Improvement in 2016,* Center for Retirement Research Issue Brief 18-1, January 2018, https://crr. bc.edu/wp-content/uploads/2018/01/IB_18-1.pdf.

advisors do not consider basic factors that contribute to the success or failure of your retirement, such as taxes, Social Security optimization, high inflation, long-term care, and longevity risk. Just putting your money in the market and hoping it grows enough to prevent you from running out of money is not enough. You may hope the money grows enough so you won't run out, but you can never be sure. That's why Retirement Renegade, my financial advising firm, specializes in the descent. We focus on helping our clients get safely down the mountain of retirement, which puts me in a unique position to cover this topic for you.

WHY PEOPLE RUN OUT OF RETIREMENT MONEY

During retirement, you want to enjoy life! It's time to relax, kick back, and coast down that mountain. But way too many people reach their golden years only to find that their money has run out. There are a lot of reasons why this happens, from fees and required minimum distributions to the state of the market and rising inflation rates. In this section, I'll cover that and some big factors that might run you dry if you're planning on retiring within the next few decades.

FEES

According to *Forbes*, the average cumulative fee for retirement accounts, including 401(k)s, 403(b)s, 457s, TSPs, and IRAs, is 2.1 percent. There can be some variance between these, but the average is 2.1 percent. Usually, that 2.1 percent is comprised of 1 to 1.5 percent for the advisor, with the rest going to expense ratios and account fees.[15] But think about it. Let's say you're sixty-five years old with a million dollars in your retirement account, and 2.1 percent of that is $21,000 a year in fees. If you live for thirty years and maintain your balance, you will pay $630,000 in fees—assuming your money doesn't grow. That's not exactly pocket change!

That doesn't even consider what you've already paid *up to* the age of sixty-five. Remember this statistic from Chapter 1? According to NerdWallet.com, the average American will spend $1.1 million in fees over their lifetime.[16] Think about it—how much traveling could you achieve with $1.1 million? How much charity or benevolence could you give with the same amount? How much could you bless your kids with $1.1 million? And yet that money is going to *fees*!

---

15 Daniel Blue, "Understanding Hidden Retirement Account Fees," *Forbes*, February 8, 2021, https://www.forbes.com/sites/forbesfinancecouncil/2021/02/08/understanding-hidden-retirement-account-fees.

16 Issa, "Financial Fees," 2018.

As you can see, fees are a significant issue, and you should try to minimize them. At my firm, Retirement Renegade, many of our offerings have zero fees because we want to put that money back in your pocket.

REQUIRED MINIMUM DISTRIBUTIONS

The vast majority of your retirement savings are probably in pre-tax accounts like IRAs, traditional 401(k)s, 403(b)s, 457s, and TSPs. Once you hit a certain age, the government forces you to take a required minimum distribution (RMD) from these pre-tax accounts so they can collect their taxes. The RMD age used to be seventy and a half. It was increased to seventy-two, and as of the writing of this book, it's seventy-three. In 2033, it will be age seventy-five.[17]

This creeping forward on the age of RMDs is dangerous. The government doesn't care if you need the money, want the money, or if the market is down. The government will simply force you to take required minimum distributions on those pre-tax accounts when you reach that certain age because they want their tax dollars. And that can become a big problem for taxes and sequence of returns risk. If the market is down and the

---

17   Greg Iacurci, "Secure 2.0 Changes 3 Key Rules Around Required
       Withdrawals from Retirement Accounts," CNBC, January 3, 2023,
       https://www.cnbc.com/2023/01/03/3-changes-in-secure-2point0-for-
       required-minimum-distributions.html.

government forces you to take a distribution anyway, you can run out of money prematurely. For example, let's say your pre-tax accounts are invested in the market, and the market happens to be down 30 percent that year. When you are forced to take out withdrawals to satisfy your RMD that year, you realize the loss by selling in a down year. If you have too many years like this, this is how you can run out of money before you run out of life. This is yet another reason why, as you learned in the last chapter, pre-tax retirement accounts are a bad idea.

THE STATE OF THE MARKET AT RETIREMENT

I've got a little story that perfectly exemplifies the importance of the state of the market when you retire. Sisters Jane and Jill both retire with $500,000 in their IRAs, and they both plan to withdraw $30,000 per year. Jane retires in the year 2000 during a strong economy, and Jill retires in 2010 during a recession. By the end of 2019, Jill has less than $100,000 saved, while Jane has almost $900,000 in her account. This $800,000 difference in savings is simply because Jane retired into a bull market (a market that is going up) while Jill retired into a bear market (a market that is going down).

TWO SISTERS,
TWO (DIFFERENT) RETIREMENTS

- $500,000 each (IRA) at retirement
- Jane will use $30,000 annually for income. } **THE RESULT?**
- Jill retired in 2010. Jane retired in 2000.

INCOME AND SEQUENCE OF RETURNS

JILL RETIRED IN 2010

END OF YEAR	MARKET RETURN	WITHDRAWAL	IRA ACCOUNT BALANCE
			$500,000
2010	12.8%	$30,000	$530,079
2011	0.0%	$30,000	$500,063
2012	13.4%	$30,000	$533,078
2013	29.6%	$30,000	$651,995
2014	11.4%	$30,000	$692,845
2015	-0.7%	$30,000	$658,028
2016	9.5%	$30,000	$687,911
2017	19.4%	$30,000	$785,677
2018	-6.2%	$30,000	$708,544
2019	28.9%	$30,000	**$874,494**

JANE RETIRED IN 2000

END OF YEAR	MARKET RETURN	WITHDRAWAL	IRA ACCOUNT BALANCE
			$500,000
2000	-10.1%	$30,000	$422,346
2001	-13.0%	$30,000	$341,173
2002	23.4%	$30,000	$238,465
2003	26.4%	$30,000	$263,459
2004	9.0%	$30,000	$254,455
2005	3.0%	$30,000	$231,190
2006	13.6%	$30,000	$228,591
2007	3.5%	$30,000	$205,601
2008	-38.5%	$30,000	$108,019
2009	23.5%	$30,000	**$96,318**

I can't overemphasize what a difference this makes. If you retire into a bull market, you're going to be fine no matter what you're invested in. However, if you retire into a bear market, your investment choices matter a lot more. The wrong choices could tank your account.

So, are you going to retire into a bear market or a bull market? Well, I keep a magic eight ball on my desk, and when clients are in my office, we shake the eight ball to find out if they'll retire into a bear market or bull market. You can come in, and I'll shake the eight ball for you if you want! All kidding aside, the point is that we don't know what the market will do. We don't have a crystal ball to predict the market's future direction as you retire. This uncertainty means your retirement relies on the flip of a coin. Hence, it's very important to have a risk reduction strategy that preserves your principal as you approach retirement.

RISING INFLATION RATE

Somewhat related to the economy is the inflation rate. If your financial advisor is factoring in a 3 percent inflation rate, they're doing you a disservice. And, by the way, they very well may be. The vast majority of advisors do not factor in the real 5 to 6 percent inflation rate we're all facing over the upcoming decades.[18] If your retirement strategy doesn't consider a realistic inflation rate, your entire portfolio is built upon a faulty premise and it will result in failure. You need to make sure to factor this in.

UNRELIABLE SOCIAL SECURITY

The next two reasons why people run out of money are a little ahead of us, but that doesn't mean we can ignore them. Remember the Social Security stopgap fund from the last chapter? This is a specific fund earmarked for when Social Security is cut by a third. When that happens, this fund can kick in and make up the difference of the lost income for the rest of your life.

If your advisor hasn't talked to you about this and even helped you create a Social Security stopgap fund, then you're being taken advantage of. This may not be because of malicious intent. Your advisor may not know what they're doing, they may not be aware of this impending reality, or they may simply not factor it into their financial plans. If you bring up this idea, they may even brush it off and say, "Oh, we'll just put your money in the market. It'll grow there."

You cannot count on that. If your advisor says this to you, you need to find another advisor. That is a defensive

---

18   Jeanna Smialek, "Inflation Cools to 5% in March, but It's a Long Road Back to Normal," *New York Times*, April 12, 2023, https://www.nytimes.com/2023/04/12/business/inflation-fed-rates.html.

plan, not an offensive plan. You need to have a specific fund to cover the gap.

A "LOST DECADE" IN 2030

Finally, we have to think about the possibility of a "lost decade." A lost decade is a period of ten years (or more) in the stock market where the average rate of return is negative. Predicting the stock market is difficult in the short term, but it's much easier in the long term. Why? Well, short-term predictions involve graphs and a lot of variables, making them very complicated. But in the long term, you can predict the market by looking at demographics.

Demographics are big-picture ideas about segmenting populations, and that gives us a lot of information. We know, for instance, that Americans between the ages of forty-five and fifty-four spend the most money.[19] We know that people between the ages of nineteen and thirty consume the most calories per day.[20] Additionally, we know that around 2030, the United States will have a swelling elderly population. Because of that, we won't have enough

---

19   "Consumer Expenditures Report 2019: BLS Reports." U.S. Bureau of Labor Statistics," December 22, 2020, https://www.bls.gov/opub/reports/consumer-expenditures/2019/home.htm.

20   "WWEIA Data Tables: USDA ARS," Accessed September 12, 2023, https://www.ars.usda.gov/northeast-area/beltsville-md-bhnrc/beltsville-human-nutrition-research-center/food-surveys-research-group/docs/wweia-data-tables/.

taxpayers to cover the rising costs of Social Security,[21] Social Security Disability, Medicare, and Medicaid, which are the vast majority of our expenditures as a country. In other words, the imbalance in funding for these programs will drag down our economy.

Unfortunately, we are not the only nation in this predicament. China is the country with the largest rate of decline in population due to aging, and Japan and Germany (along with a few other European countries) aren't far behind.[22] There is an old saying that "as Germany goes, so goes Europe." And finally, Japan has the worst aging demographics in the entire world.[23] Between four of the global superpowers—America, China, Germany, and Japan—this predicament is just enough to affect the entire global economy. We may end up having a "lost decade" similar to what we had from 2000 to 2013, where the S&P had a negative return. This is not fearmongering; this is based on the numbers.

If we indeed have a "lost decade" around 2030, what will that do to your retirement account? If the market

21   "How Will Boomers Affect Social Security?," National Academy of Social Insurance, accessed November 21, 2023, https://www.nasi.org/learn/social-security/how-will-boomers-affect-social-security/.

22   Euronews and AFP, "The Countries Where Population Is Declining," *Euronews*, January 20, 2023, https://www.euronews.com/2023/01/17/the-countries-where-population-is-declining.

23   "Countries with the Oldest Populations in the World," Population Reference Bureau, accessed November 21, 2023, Accessed September 12, 2023, https://www.prb.org/resources/countries-with-the-oldest-populations-in-the-world/.

totally stagnates between 2030 to 2040, will that affect your retirement plan? Absolutely! That's why it's essential to protect and insulate yourself from a potential "lost decade." How can you do that? Reduce your risk.

GETTING RID OF THE NIGHT SWEATS BY REDUCING RISK

Lots of people find themselves constantly worrying about their financial situation. Maybe it's keeping you up at night. You might get a sick feeling in your stomach when you hear news about the market crashing 600 points. This used to be me. I was very athletic in my twenties, but I would have fainting spells at work because of stress (and too much caffeine)! Stress can lead to chronic illness and premature death, as you learned in the last chapter. So when it comes to your money, it's important to have a stress-free retirement. The last thing you need is a bunch of stress that can kill you off earlier than expected. With safety, security, and peace of mind wrapped around your retirement, you can live longer and happier.

Then again, some folks have the complete opposite issue. We had the greatest bull market in American history in the 2010s, and a lot of people had a good experience growing their money during that time. Now they're torn because they're facing a big dilemma. They know that they've done well because of the market, but as they get closer to retirement, they realize that they have grown addicted to investing. They check their phones and see what the market has done over the last week, and they love the thrill of finding and exploiting a good investment. If this is you, maybe it's time to use a poker analogy: Take your earnings off the poker table and cash in. You've done well, but leave while you're ahead! You can no longer afford to take risks like that now that you're about to count on those funds to survive.

Whether you're an investing daredevil or prefer to hide all your cash in your mattress, there's a great stress test you can take to help you make sure you're on the right track. This test can help you determine the amount you're comfortable losing. That way, you can squirrel away everything else in a safe and secure investment (not your mattress) while still participating in the market. This will allow you to enjoy your retirement without any financial worries.

There's only one simple question on this test: Out of your total investable assets, how much would you feel comfortable losing?

Let's say you have two million dollars saved up, and you're not sure how much risk to take. If you're not comfortable losing any money, it's time to move your investments to something safer. But, if you're comfortable losing, say, 75 percent, then you can put 25 percent of your money into something safe and growing—something that won't lose value. You can pick safer options like fixed indexed annuities or hybrid CDs that guarantee preservation of principal through a contractual agreement. So take the stress test and see what percentage of risk is the right fit for you!

LOW-RISK INVESTMENT OPTIONS: THE POWER OF INSURANCE

Once you've figured out the total amount you're unwilling to lose, you need to figure out what safe investments can protect it. The three options in this section can provide a secure financial future for you, and they all have something important in common: They rely on insurance companies rather than banks.

A lot of people have never heard of fixed index annuities, hybrid CDs, and living benefits through a life insurance chassis. Others have only heard of them in passing. There's a simple reason for this: People who sell them don't make nearly as much commission on these products as they do on putting your money in the market and charging fees. But although most people have never considered these, they are incredible options that check off many of your retirement boxes. We will explore each option in detail to help you secure that percentage of your liquid investable assets in retirement, but first, let's address why investments built on insurance are such a good idea.

THE INCREASING VOLATILITY OF BANKS

You might have noticed that banks are getting increasingly volatile. For every ten cents they have in deposits, banks are allowed by state and federal law to lend or leverage *fourteen times* the deposits they have![24] Banks fail all the time and have to be merged, acquired, or bailed out by bigger banks. Since 2008, 22 percent of US banks have had to do this because of bad loans, liquidity problems, and so on.[25] It happens all the time.

In contrast, since 1900, there have been over 6,000 insurance companies,[26] and compared to banks, A-rated annuity companies typically have zero contagion risk, higher substitutability, and near-zero financial vulnerability. Their financial position deteriorates at a much slower rate compared to banks. That explains why their rate of failure and bankruptcy is way lower than that

---

24 "United States Reserve Requirement Ratio," CEIC, July 10, 2020, https://www.ceicdata.com/en/indicator/united-states/reserve-requirement-ratio.

25 Federal Deposit Insurance Corporation (FDIC), *Crisis and Response: An FDIC History, 2008–2013* (Washington, DC: FDIC, 2017).

26 Mark Richard Greene, "Insurance: Definition, History, Types, Companies, & Facts," Encyclopedia Britannica, updated November 16, 2023, https://www.britannica.com/topic/insurance/historical-development-of-insurance.

of banks.[27] In fact, since 1900, not one A-rated life and annuity insurance company has failed. (Property and casualty companies are in a completely different class and are much more vulnerable than life and annuity companies. Property and casualty companies fail all the time, as they are not required to keep surplus solvency above their liabilities.)

This is because the life and annuity insurance company model is the opposite of the banking model. These insurance companies are required to keep surplus cash on hand to avoid failure. (Quick definition: An annuity is a financial product that provides a regular stream of income over a specified period, sort of like a personal pension plan.)

Keep in mind that property and casualty insurance companies are a completely different ballgame; those companies fail all the time due to natural disasters. But a life insurance and annuity company is secure. It is required to keep surplus investments very liquid. In fact, they often have to keep a very high solvency percentage to abide by state and federal laws and regulations. So if there were to be some sort of liquidity crisis or cash crisis, an annuity company is the last domino to fall.

Take Allianz, for example. Allianz, one of the annuity companies I like, is a trillion-dollar company that

27 "Why Insurers Differ from Banks," Insurance Europe, October 2014, https://www.insuranceeurope.eu/publications/488/why-insurers-differ-from-banks/.

has been around since the 1800s.[28] Allianz has the most popular annuity of all time as well as the biggest-increasing income annuity in all of North America. It is the third-largest diversified insurance company in the world[29] and the ninth-largest asset manager in the world.[30] They are a $1 trillion company with a 105.5 percent solvency ratio, which means if they paid out everybody tomorrow—all of their liabilities, all of their IOUs, the people they owe money to—they'd have $55 billion in cash left over. They avoid investing in China, and often their products have zero fees, liquidity, and increasing income. You get all that with an institution that has a proven track record, having survived two World Wars, the Korean War, the Great Depression, multiple global financial crises, the dot-com bubble, COVID-19, and more.

It's no wonder the top five banks invest their money heavily in life insurance and annuity companies! These companies are the safest institutions in the world. All of the banks would fail before the insurance companies failed.

In addition, annuities have their own version of Federal Deposit Insurance Corporation (FDIC) insurance

28 Jennifer Schell and Chip Stapleton, "Allianz Life," Annuity.org, updated November 17, 2023, https://www.annuity.org/annuities/providers/allianz-life/.

29 Mark Rosanes, "These Are the World's 20 Largest Insurance Companies in 2022," *Insurance Business America*, September 23, 2022, https://www.insurancebusinessmag.com/us/guides/these-are-the-worlds-20-largest-insurance-companies-in-2022-421548.aspx.

30 "World's Top Asset Management Firms," ADV Ratings, updated June 30, 2023, https://www.advratings.com/top-asset-management-firms.

called the State Guarantee Association. Every company has its own version of FDIC, which covers typically between $250,000 and $300,000 per insurance carrier, per person. So there's another level of protection if an annuity company happens to fail. Most A-rated annuity companies, however, don't even need insurance because they have so much financial strength. Even so, it is a nice little cherry on top to have that extra version of FDIC insurance.

Now that you understand just how secure these investments are, let's get into your options.

FIXED INDEX ANNUITIES

I mentioned fixed index annuities briefly in the previous chapter as an important part of your silo, but I want to go over them in much more detail here because they are a cornerstone of risk reduction. Statistics show that there were over $310 billion in fixed indexed annuity sales in America in 2022 alone.[31] In 2023, fixed indexed annuity sales in America are on track to hit $360 billion.[32] This number has been growing as more and more people recognize the utility and value of fixed index annuities.

---

31 "LIMRA: 2022 U.S. Retail Annuity Sales Shatter Annual Sales Records Set in 2008," LIMRA, January 26, 2023, https://www.limra.com/en/newsroom/news-releases/2023/limra-2022-u.s.-retail-annuity-sales-shatter-annual-sales-records-set-in-2008/.

32 Gregg Greenberg, "Record demand for RILAs pushes Q3 annuity sales to new heights," *Investment News*, October 25, 2023, https://www.investmentnews.com/record-demand-for-rilas-pushes-q3-annuity-sales-to-new-heights-244864.

Investors are fleeing the market to put their money in something secure. They want a guaranteed rate of return or potential market upside without the downside, high fees, and risk of market volatility. Fidelity, Morgan Stanley, Wells Fargo, Merrill Lynch, and Citibank all recommend annuities as part of your portfolio at the time of writing. Even Dave Ramsey and Suze Orman have endorsed fixed indexed annuities recently. They are changing their minds on annuities due to the evolution of annuities being increasingly competitive alternatives to a volatile market.

Annuities from twenty to thirty years ago got a bad rap, and for good reason: They were not very competitive. They had high fees and very little liquidity provisions. Also, in many cases, if you died, the insurance company would keep the death benefit. Talk about a bad deal! Fast-forward to today; now these products offer incredible rates of returns, zero fees, liquidity provision, long-term care benefits, and very strong death benefits. There are still bad annuities. In fact, there are nine different kinds of annuities. Our firm recommends only three out of those nine. From those three different types of annuities, we offer over 1,200 products from the top seventy-five financial companies in the United States.

Fixed index annuities are a wonderful tool to provide you with an increasing income in retirement that offsets inflation. You can participate in market upside without the downside. There are often few fees (sometimes zero fees), they still have liquidity, and they are guaranteed through one of the safest institutions in the world: insurance companies.

BEWARE OF VARIABLE ANNUITIES

If you pay any attention to big names in finance, annuities may initially make you nervous. Financial entertainers like Dave Ramsey, Suze Orman, Rick Edelman, and Ken Fisher regularly cast aspersions against annuities (often variable annuities), and they have a valid argument. There are good annuities and bad annuities. For example, I am not a big fan of variable annuities. And guess what? When those financial entertainers lambaste annuities, they are often referring to variable annuities, not fixed index annuities.

Here's a quick crash course. Fixed index annuities and variable annuities are both types of annuities (insurance contracts) that provide investors with regular payments. The key difference between the two is how they invest the premiums paid by the investor. Fixed index annuities invest the premiums in a fixed index, such as the S&P 500, with a guaranteed minimum interest rate. This means that the investor can benefit from market growth while avoiding market losses. But the more controversial variable annuities invest the premiums in mutual funds, allowing for greater potential returns, but they also carry greater risk. The value of the variable annuity fluctuates with the performance of the underlying mutual funds. Since the point of this section is reducing risk, variable annuities aren't a great fit.

To make matters worse, variable annuities have some of the highest fees in the investment world.[33] You'll pay, on average, 3.5 to 5.5 percent in fees each year on these accounts, which is ludicrous.[34] You can still lose your principal, and there are high surrender charges. This is part of the reason why variable annuities have been declining in sales over the years.

Plus, variable annuities sometimes come with an income rider, which guarantees a minimum level of income for life. That may sound good, but when the income rider is turned on, it stays "flat," which means the guaranteed minimum income amount will not increase, even if the underlying investments in the annuity perform well. Finally, variable annuities don't grow each year to help offset inflation. So if you're looking into annuities, stick to fixed index annuities.

---

33   ABC News, "The Pros and Many Cons of Variable Annuities," *ABC News*, August 25, 2015, https://abcnews.go.com/Business/pros-cons-variable-annuities/story?id=33229630.

34   Tara Siegel Bernard, "Variable Annuity Plus Guaranteed Income Merits Careful Scrutiny," *The New York Times*, June 19, 2015, https://www.nytimes.com/2015/06/20/your-money/variable-annuities-with-guaranteed-income-riders-require-careful-scrutiny.html.

HYBRID CDS

The hybrid certificate of deposit (CD) is a product that is built upon an annuity chassis. Think of an annuity chassis as the framework or structure on which an annuity is built. It's the foundation that supports the annuity's features and benefits.

A hybrid CD is essentially a special type of certificate of deposit that provides you with a guaranteed rate of return that is higher than any bank offers. Plus, these CDs are issued by an insurance company that's safer than every bank in America. They have the added advantage of allowing you to maintain liquidity. If you remove your money from a traditional CD, you surrender all your interest. With a hybrid CD, you can often remove 10 percent per year while still enjoying that guaranteed rate of return in the safest institutions in the world!

LIVING BENEFITS THROUGH A LIFE INSURANCE CHASSIS

Our final insurance-based investment option is living benefits through a life insurance chassis. These can provide you with total liquidity, and starting from day one, you get a multiple on your money as a death benefit. A multiple is basically a factor by which your money is multiplied when it is paid out as a death benefit. In other words, the death benefit amount you receive is higher than the original amount of money you put in. For instance, if you invested $100,000, you may have $400,000 to $500,000 as a death benefit with long-term care benefits. It's a pretty good deal.

There are other advantages to living benefits as well. Your money goes up if the market increases, but if it crashes, you don't lose a penny. There are various long-term care benefits, including products that offer tax-free benefits. For example, you have a tax-free death benefit if you pass away. This makes living benefits a great pick for risk-averse retirees.

DON'T RISK YOUR RETIREMENT

Financial risks are fine when you're younger and have time to bounce back, but as you get closer to retirement, it is essential that you change your game plan. What worked in preseason does not work in the Super Bowl. The strategy that worked in high school softball is not going to work in the Major Leagues. The Sherpa's approach to getting you up Mount Everest won't work so well on the descent.

The approach you've been utilizing for the last twenty, thirty, or forty years has served you well, but now you require a different strategy as you enter the decumulation years of life. I hope this chapter helped you get an idea of how to rid yourself of financial risk and ensure a secure retirement. Taking a look at the potential pitfalls that can lead to running out of money, such as high fees, market volatility, rising inflation, and the uncertainties surrounding Social Security, can help you plan around them. Choosing insurance-driven investments, like fixed index annuities, hybrid CDs, or living benefits offered through a life insurance chassis, can protect your savings and help you live out your retirement in style.

The investment strategy outlined in this chapter will get you safely down that mountain. However, everyone's financial needs are different, and it's crucial that you get the guidance, expertise, and wisdom you need to have the happy, safe, and flourishing retirement you deserve. We offer a free fifteen-minute phone consultation to get your specific questions answered. You can simply go to www. retirementrenegade.com to request your free, no-obligation consultation so you can know how to set your retirement up for guaranteed success!

3

DON'T TIP THE IRS

Benjamin Franklin, an American polymath and one of the Founding Fathers of the United States, wrote, "In this world nothing can be said to be certain, except death and taxes."[35] And that is indeed true. It is what it is—taxes are not something that we can really get away from. The system is set up to take from what we earn.

Of course, there are ways you can minimize taxes, but even those tactics are shifting. Taxes for many pretax or tax-deferred accounts changed in 2020 with the Secure Act, and the benefits of deferring taxes in these accounts significantly diminished. You used to be able to defer taxes almost indefinitely, but that has changed.[36] It's important

35   Benjamin Franklin to Jean Baptiste Le Roy, "On the Affairs of France," November 13, 1789, in *The Private Correspondence of Benjamin Franklin*, 2nd. ed., vol. 1, edited by William Temple Franklin (London: Henry Colburn, 1817), 266.

36   Ephie Coumanakos, "SECURE Act Basics: What Everyone Should Know," *Kiplinger*, March 24, 2020, https://www.kiplinger.com/article/retirement/t037-c032-s014-secure-act-basics-what-everyone-should-know.html.

to understand how the current tax situation affects you and how you can leverage it as much as possible.

In this chapter, we'll first delve into the reality that you don't actually own as much as you might think, especially when it comes to your retirement savings, thanks to rising tax rates. Then I'll show you how to minimize your retirement tax bill so you don't end up with a nasty surprise just when you're ready to relax. With some knowledge of the different ways retirement accounts are taxed, you can do a lot to reduce your tax bill and keep as much of your hard-won funds as you possibly can.

YOU DON'T OWN AS MUCH AS YOU THINK

As William Feather said, "The reward of energy, enterprise, and thrift is taxes."[37] You may be looking at your $1 million or $2 million or $500,000 portfolio and feeling accomplished, as you should. But although it may say $2 million on your bank statement, a substantial portion of that does not belong to you. A lot of that actually belongs to the government, and the government wants it ASAP.

In this section, I'll show you just how much taxes can cut into your retirement savings and whatever you want to leave to your heirs. We'll also take a look at the future trajectory of taxes, including the ones that pertain to that

---

37 William Feather, *The Business of Life* (New York: Simon and Schuster, 1949).

individual retirement account (IRA) you've been carefully growing for decades. Finally, we'll tackle the difference between saving in pretax versus nonqualified vehicles, which can have a significant effect on your tax bill.

THE IRA IS AN IOU TO THE IRS

Whenever I conduct a workshop or give a presentation, I mention either Trump or Jesus. It's kind of funny how much these two words immediately divide the audience. It's a lighthearted thing I do to observe people's reactions, but I don't do it just to get a rise out of people. This comes up in tax seminars because, love him or hate him, Trump passed tax reform in 2017 that significantly benefited middle-class Americans.[38] The law stipulates that taxes will go back up at the end of 2025, though.[39] According to experts, it's highly likely that we will experience a 30 percent tax increase in 2026, possibly returning to the tax rates and style of the 1990s.[40]

---

38 Justin Haskins, "IRS Data Proves Trump Tax Cuts Benefited Middle, Working-Class Americans Most," The Hill, December 4, 2021, https:// thehill.com/opinion/finance/584190-irs-data-prove-trump-tax-cuts-benefited-middle-working-class-americans-most/.

39 Kathleen Coxwell, "TCJA and 2026 Tax Brackets: Why Your Taxes Are Likely to Increase and What to Do About It," NewRetirement, June 30, 2022, https://www.newretirement.com/retirement/2026-tax-brackets-tcja-expiration/.

40 Tax Policy Center. "Analysis of the Tax Cuts and Jobs Act," Accessed September 12, 2023 https://www.taxpolicycenter.org/feature/analysis-tax-cuts-and-jobs-act.

One study examined the impact of taxing the top 1 percent of income earners in America at 100 percent revealed that such a measure would only cover the country's expenses for seven months.[41] *Seven months!* This illustrates that our issue is not a tax problem, but rather a spending problem. Unfortunately, there seems to be no end in sight to the escalating amount of money being spent. The problem keeps compounding, especially thanks to interest on the substantial debt we owe. Consequently, taxes will increase; the government doesn't really have a choice.

This brings me to my next point: An IRA is essentially an IOU to the IRS.

PRETAX ACCOUNTS AND RISING TAXES: A DANGEROUS COMBINATION

Suppose I approached you and proposed that we start an ice cream shop in your hometown. They need another ice cream shop in town, and it's clear you have the expertise to run one successfully. You are skilled in managing the storefront, while I can handle the backend business operations and bookkeeping. Together, we can provide a valuable service to our community. Imagine I say to you, "Don't worry about paying me for now. I'll just keep track, and

---

41   Patricia Cohen, "What Could Raising Taxes on the 1% Do? Surprising Amounts," *New York Times*, June 8, 2021, https://www.nytimes.com/2015/10/17/business/putting-numbers-to-a-tax-increase-for-the-rich.html.

down the road, I'll tell you how much you owe me. At that point, you'll have to pay me whatever amount I say you owe. Sound good?" Your answer would likely be, "Heck *no*!" But if you have a pretax account, that's essentially the deal you've made with the government.

You might remember this from Chapter 1: Many people have saved up a comfortable nest egg and feel good about going into retirement. They look at their seven-figure portfolio and figure they've got plenty of money to get them through retirement. Maybe this is you, and if you're like most folks, the majority of your cash is in pretax accounts like traditional IRAs, 401(k)s, 403(b)s, 457s, TSPs, and so on. If that's the case, the number on the screen can be very deceptive.

If you're retiring within the next five to ten years or are already retired, you probably had it hammered into your head that you should defer taxes in certain accounts. As I mentioned before, this idea was based on the belief that you'd be in a lower tax bracket during retirement. Everybody bought into this idea: Defer taxes while making more money and then pay them when your tax bracket is lower in retirement.

However, as you now know, it's highly likely that your tax bracket may remain the same or even increase after retirement. Because the IRS is raising taxes, they're essentially boosting you up that tax bracket ladder sooner, even when you're retired. You're basically going into business with the IRS, which is telling you, "Hey, don't worry about paying us now. We'll just keep track of your taxes, and down the road, we'll tell you how much you owe us. At that point, you'll have to pay us whatever amount we say you owe." This is not a good idea!

When you are retired, you are actually paying just as much, if not more, in taxes as you were before. As a result, you end up paying more in taxes during retirement than you would have while working! That completely contradicts the purpose and premise of what you were initially led to believe. This is a big problem. On top of that, as I just mentioned, the rates for each bracket will likely increase. Taxes have to go up because we have over $32 trillion in debt at the time of writing, and that number increases by the day.[42] We don't know how much your IOU will be for. The government could claim you owe them some exorbitant amount down the road, and that is dangerous.

IRAs AND INHERITANCE

Pretax accounts don't just screw *you* over, they can get your kids too. As of today, if your kids inherit a pretax traditional IRA, 401(k), 403(b), 457, etc., they will have to draw down that account over ten years. The income they take

---

42 "Human Rights," *Firing Line* broadcast records, March 9, 1977, Hoover Institution Library & Archives, https://digitalcollections.hoover.org/objects/6450/human-rights.

will be taxed as ordinary income, and usually when the parents pass away, the kids are in their peak earning years. They may be in the 22 percent, 24 percent, or even the 32 percent tax bracket. They may lose anywhere from 30 to 40 percent of that to taxes depending on how much they make. That's a big bummer for them.

KNOW WHAT YOU'RE UP AGAINST: TAX-SAVING RETIREMENT STRATEGIES

When clients first come into my office, we often run a tax report for them. Upon crunching the numbers, they are usually shocked to realize how much they'll pay in taxes due to required minimum distributions. If there is money left over for their children to inherit, the taxes their children will pay can also add up. Sometimes this eats up the entire value of the account. If they have a million-dollar account, they may end up paying over a million dollars in taxes throughout their lifetime and leaving your children nothing. That's insane. Luckily, there is something you can do about it.

Taking a closer look at your options, including post-tax and nonqualified vehicles and their effects on inheritance, can go a long way toward getting those taxes under control. Know, too, that all is not lost if you're approaching retirement (or are already retired) with your retirement funds tied up in pretax accounts. You now know what you're up against, so you can now take steps to give the IRS less.

PRETAX, POST-TAX, AND NONQUALIFIED VEHICLES

You are likely aware that there are a bunch of different types of retirement accounts, and many of them are taxed differently. Pretax, post-tax, and nonqualified vehicles are three ways in which retirement accounts can be taxed. Here's a closer look at these different tax methods and how each one can affect how much you end up with.

EMPLOYER-SPONSORED PRETAX ACCOUNTS

At this point, you probably won't be shocked to learn that I recommend avoiding any sort of pretax accounts such as 401(k)s, IRAs, 403(b)s, 457s, or TSPs. This is because the pretax vehicles are not as competitive as they used to be before the Secure Act changed the rules in 2020. In other words, the benefits of saving in pre-tax vehicles have largely diminished. You're just left with a massive ticking tax time bomb that will hurt you massively down the road.

That being said, sometimes you can't avoid pretax accounts. What if saving in pretax is the primary option your employer recommends? Should you still avoid it? The answer is maybe, maybe not. You can take advantage of any employer match because whatever your employer matches is a 100 percent gain. However, if your employer offers a Roth option, definitely take the Roth option. As of the time of writing, Roth matching is allowed because of the Secure Act 2.0 that passed in December 2022. Yes, you can actually get matching contributions to a Roth nowadays! If the 401(k) is your only option, take advantage of the 401(k) match and then max out your own Roth contributions for the year. Once you have done this, I recommend saving all of the rest of your money in post-tax accounts. You will not be able to deduct it from your income that year, but you will ultimately pay less money in taxes in the long run.

TAX-FREE AND NONQUALIFIED (POST-TAX) VEHICLES

If pretax accounts are a bad idea, naturally, you may be wondering about tax-free, or nonqualified (post-tax), accounts. The Roth IRA is an example of a tax-free account; you pay taxes before the money goes in, and then you own 100 percent of what's in the account tax-free. Plus, any growth is tax-free.

You also have the option of investing in nonqualified or post-tax accounts. They include brokerage accounts, regular savings accounts, or even real estate investments outside of dedicated retirement accounts. Of course, when you invest in accounts like this, you do so with post-tax dollars. In other words, you don't get any tax deductions up front for contributing to these accounts. This also means you won't end up owing Uncle Sam a massive check down the line.

The main advantage of nonqualified accounts is flexibility. You can withdraw your contributions at any time without penalties or restrictions since you've already paid taxes on that money. However, any investment gains or income generated within the account may be subject to taxes *in the year they are earned.* This is known as capital gains tax or dividend tax, depending on the type of income.

Unlike taxes on tax-deferred accounts, and depending on the types of vehicles you invest in, you pay these taxes every year, and you only pay them on gains. Sometimes you do not have to pay these capital gains until you withdraw the money. Plus, the tax rates for these gains are typically lower than ordinary income tax rates.

When it comes to inheritance, Roth or nonqualified/post-tax money is also the best to inherit, while pretax is the worst.

For the pretax accounts, the kids still have to draw the inherited accounts down over ten years and pay ordinary income taxes on the withdrawal. If your children inherit a post-tax or nonqualified account, such as stocks, bonds, or mutual funds, they not only avoid taxes but also don't have to draw the funds down over ten years either. If they inherit Roth accounts, they will have to draw down the accounts over ten years, but they will pay no taxes.

So, to recap, my advice is not to invest in pretax accounts (traditional IRAs, 401(k)s, etc.) if you can avoid it. Pay the taxes now while they're lower so that down the road, you (or your kids) don't end up with a giant tax bill. You can do this via a Roth account or a nonqualified account, which I'd be happy to help with.

IS A ROTH CONVERSION RIGHT FOR YOU?

What if you're stuck with a bunch of pre-tax retirement accounts? You might not be feeling so great about that right now. Depending on your situation, Roth conversions can be an amazing way to convert some of your pre-tax money to tax-free money. Sometimes, this is known as a backdoor Roth conversion (or a backdoor Roth, for short).

A Roth conversion allows you to convert a traditional IRA to a Roth. The problem is you have to pay the taxes up front, and often it's a big chunk of money. If it will benefit your financial standing to go ahead with the conversion, it's best to pay the taxes from a post-tax account, such as a checking or savings account. That being said, from my observations, Roth conversions are only a good fit for everyday Americans about half the time. Sometimes the juice is not worth the squeeze, and you just have to deal with the IRA—with taxes from your pretax accounts.

Don't make the mistake of converting when it won't benefit you. You can only figure it out by considering your whole financial picture. That's why you need to check with an advisor and have them run a tax report to see whether it's a prudent strategy. If your advisor did not proactively do this for you in the beginning, give us a call and we will run a Roth conversion tax report for you for free.

CONCLUSION

Economist Milton Friedman once said, "We have a system that increasingly taxes work and subsidizes nonwork."[43] You may have worked hard on your savings, but that won't stop the government from taking their share! Taxes are on the rise, and pretax accounts like IRAs can get taxed pretty aggressively. By understanding pretax, post-tax, and nonqualified vehicles, including their effect on inheritance, you can make a smart decision for yourself and your family. Depending on your situation, a Roth conversion can also help if your money is mostly tied up in those tricky pretax accounts.

You don't want to lose 30 to 40 percent of your nest egg in taxes, so it's important to meet with an advisor to

---

43   "Human Rights." *Firing Line*, hosted by William F. Buckley Jr., featuring Allard K. Lowenstein, aired March 9, 1977, on PBS.

see whether you're on the right track. A good advisor can look at your full financial picture and determine whether there are any strategic steps you can take to manage taxes in retirement.

4

YOU NEED
REAL ESTATE DEBT

Marshall Field, an American entrepreneur and founder of
the eponymous department store, had an interesting way
of viewing real estate. He wrote, "Buying real estate is not
only the best way, the quickest way, the safest way, but the
only way to become wealthy."[44] Yes, you read that right:
Field said that buying real estate is the *only way* to become
wealthy. Interesting!

US Secretary of State William Jennings Bryan also
weighed in on real estate, saying, "Real estate is the best
investment for small savings. *More money is made from the
rise in real estate values than from all other causes combined.*"[45]
That is *so interesting*. Why did these two successful guys
believe this? Well, because it's true! Of all millionaires,

---

44   Federal Trade Commission, *Federal Trade Commission Decisions: Volume
     105* (Washington, DC: Federal Trade Commission, 1986), 112.

45   "Invest Your Money in Land," *Pearson's Magazine*, Volume 26, 1911. p
     528.

90 percent made their money primarily in real estate.[46] Additionally, more wealth is accumulated in real estate than in any other category combined.[47] That's why you need to get in on this and own real estate.

Obviously, Secretary Jennings and Mr. Field provided some pretty compelling reasons why real estate is a crucial investment. But in this chapter, I'm going to share a little more about real estate investments. First, we'll explore the concept of good debt versus bad debt and how it relates to real estate. Then we'll dive into the many benefits of real estate investments, which largely center around one very compelling concept: lower taxes.

GOOD DEBT VERSUS BAD DEBT

We're used to thinking about debt as bad. What if I told you, though, that there's such a thing as good debt? If someone takes out a loan to fund their start-up, and that start-up goes on to earn billions, you could hardly consider the initial debt "bad," right?

The distinction between good debt and bad debt ultimately boils down to two things: (a) an appreciating

---

46   "Top 7 Reasons Why 90% of US Millionaires Invest in Real Estate & Why You Should Follow the Lead," Red Oak Development Group, August 3, 2022, https://redoakvc.com/top-7-reasons-why-90-of-us-millionaires-invest-in-real-estate-why-you-should-follow-the-lead.

47   David Greene, "Why Real Estate Builds Wealth More Consistently Than Other Asset Classes," *Forbes*, November 27, 2018, https://www.forbes.com/sites/davidgreene/2018/11/27/why-real-estate-builds-wealth-more-consistently-than-other-asset-classes/?sh=896d17054056.

asset and (b) positive cash flow. As you know, income is queen! Anything that will help you generate income by (a) appreciating in value over time and (b) making money on a regular basis is worth taking on debt for.

For example, if I take out a $100,000 loan and buy a brand-new, tricked-out truck, I'd be accruing bad debt. That truck's value depreciates over time, yet I still have to make monthly payments until the loan is paid off. But what if I take out that $100,000 loan and, instead of buying a fancy truck, I purchase a $400,000 rental property? Once I use the loan to pay expenses, mortgage, insurance, and taxes, as long as I generate a net cash flow of $1,000 per month, that's good debt. The $400,000 property appreciates in value over time and generates positive cash flow, along with certain tax benefits, which I'll get into in the next section.

However, it's important to note that not all real estate debt is the same or created equal. A lot of people pay the minimum on the mortgage of their primary residence because it has a low interest rate, for instance. But if you're living in the property, you're not generating income at present or in the near future. Therefore, if your only real estate investment is your primary residence, I strongly advise you to work toward paying off your mortgage by the time you retire. This approach not only provides peace of mind but also lowers your monthly expenses, since you won't have a mortgage to pay during retirement.

A WORD OF CAUTION ABOUT CREDIT CARDS

Credit card debt is one of the most insidious forms of bad debt. It does the opposite of generate income—it bleeds out your bank account with the notoriously predatory two-digit interest rates. There are two main reasons people end up in credit card debt: They are either genuinely poor or are living above their means. If someone can afford basic food and shelter for their family and they are still in credit card debt, the culprit is likely the latter.

I know we all hear this all the time, but if you don't have the cash to pay for something, it's important not to overextend yourself. You have to set up a budget that allows you to pay your mortgage, utilities, car loan, and other necessary expenses comfortably. If your income supports a used Honda Accord and a $1,000 monthly mortgage, you shouldn't be driving a brand-new, leased Tesla and paying $4,000 per month on a McMansion mortgage. That way, you won't be in a position where your budget is in the red every month.

Many of the kinds of charges people put on credit cards—takeout, airline tickets, or designer shoes—definitely aren't necessities, and they're definitely not appreciating assets that produce positive cash flow. You have to be disciplined enough to not put more on your credit cards than you have on hand for discretionary spending. Personally, I use a credit card for the sake of earning points, but I make sure to pay it off in full every month. If you find yourself unable to pay off your credit cards each month, it's best to cut them up. And if you're trying to purchase a "good debt" investment, it's best not to use a credit card for that. Seek out a loan with a lower interest rate instead.

PRIMARY RESIDENCE VERSUS RENTAL PROPERTY: DO I NEED BOTH?

It is foolish to think that real estate doesn't need to be part of your portfolio in some manner. However, real estate is very flexible—there are so many different niches you can specialize in. I recommend having rentals, whether they are short term or long term, including options like Airbnbs or lease-to-own properties. Even if you have just a couple of rentals, the benefits are massive.

Looking back at Chapter 1 again, a big part of funding a successful retirement lies in the four silos. Rental property helps a lot with the second silo: income. You know your income needs to support you throughout your retirement, and your retirement could span three or four decades—or even more, if you retire early and eat your vegetables. I recommend allocating 50 to 70 percent of your retirement savings to this silo.

That being said, sometimes the only real estate you own is your primary residence. It may not be as good as owning rental properties, but owning your primary residence is one key to financial stability. Luckily, any real estate investment can help with the third and fourth silos: growth and estate planning.

You might remember that I recommend allocating anywhere from 10 to 20 percent of your savings toward growth. This category encompasses both short-term and long-term growth opportunities, which you can then save for future expenses. This can include stuff like an anticipated major trip, saving up for a new car, planning for a child's or grandchild's college education, or even buying real estate like a new lake house. If your real estate investments do well, you can sell them off and use the funds to get that vacation home or the round-the-world trip you really want.

Finally, we've got the fourth silo: your long-term care or death benefit. If you fall ill and need to move into a nursing home, your real estate assets can fund your care, even if it gets pricey. When you do pass away, real estate assets also form a big part of your estate and allow you to leave a nice nest egg to your loved ones, often tax-free.

As you can see, real estate, whether rental properties or just your house, can be incredibly beneficial for providing long-term growth and stability in your portfolio.

Rental properties cover more silos, but simply being a homeowner covers some of them. However, that's not the only great thing about real estate investments; in fact, we're just getting started.

THE MANY TAX BENEFITS OF RENTAL REAL ESTATE

Real estate investments can cover (at least partially) three out of four silos in the Silo Strategy, and they are a proven way to increase your wealth, health, and general happiness. As if that's not enough of a reason to invest in real estate, Uncle Sam favors this type of investment with all kinds of tax breaks. There are various deductions and other tax benefits you can benefit from by using real estate. You already know not to tip the IRS, so here are more ways real estate can take even more off that tax bill. Since renting property is a form of doing business, many of these deductions are similar to the deductions of a business owner.

Keep in mind that these deductions apply only if you're using your real estate for rental property; they won't apply to your primary home. If you earn income through rental properties, house flipping, or any other real estate activity, you could be eligible for these. Also, keep in mind that real estate tax deductions can get complicated. Before you try to use these, you have to consult with a tax professional or financial planner who can help you understand the specific eligibility criteria and provide strategies to maximize your deduction. Remember: Tax mistakes can land you in jail—not the ideal way to spend your retirement!

DEDUCTIONS

You're probably already familiar with tax deductions, which can lower the amount of income you're taxed on. You can subtract these deductions from your taxable income, reducing the overall tax burden. There are five main allowable deductions for real estate, which I'll highlight here.

OPERATING EXPENSES

Operating expenses for rental real estate aren't cheap. They can include maintenance costs, property taxes, insurance premiums, and utilities, which can accumulate over time. However, these operating expenses are tax deductible, and they can lead to significant savings when it's time to file your taxes.

Imagine you own a rental property, and you want to make sure it's pretty and functions well for your tenants. You dump money into repairs and maintenance, such as fixing leaky pipes and repainting walls. You also have monthly bills for utilities like water, electricity, and heating to pay. You keep careful track of these expenses, and when tax season arrives, your accountant calculates their total and deducts them from your operating costs. This deduction reduces the overall expenses associated with running your rental.

I'll be using a hypothetical investment for this section of a $300,000 real estate investment property. Let's assume your total annual operating expenses amount to $10,000. You can deduct this $10,000 from your taxable income.

MORTGAGE INTEREST

Nobody likes paying mortgage interest, but at least it's deductible. If you've taken out a loan to finance an investment property, the interest you pay on that mortgage can be subtracted from your taxable income. Let's say you put $60,000 down on your $300,000 investment property. To pay for the rest, you took out a thirty-year loan for $240,000 with an annual interest rate of 5 percent. This means you would pay $7,456 in interest annually, and the mortgage interest deduction could provide you with a tax savings of $2,385.

DEPRECIATION

Sure, real estate goes up in value over time, but the actual structures tend to wear out and need replacement over time. The depreciation deduction accounts for this, allowing you to subtract the decline in value that properties experience over time due to wear and tear. In the

United States, most residential rental property is depreciated at a rate of 3.636 percent annually for 27.5 years.

Let's take a look at how this affects our hypothetical rental property. At the average depreciation rate, you can deduct around $10,909 ($300,000 divided by 27.5) as depreciation expense annually! That can make a *big* difference in your tax bill.

OWNER EXPENSES

Yet another deduction for real estate owners is owner expenses. When renting out property, you may incur various costs, such as property management fees, advertising expenses, or professional services like legal and accounting fees. These expenses can be deducted from your taxable income, chipping that tax bill down even more.

Let's say you incur $10,000 in owner expenses throughout the year. You can deduct these expenses from your taxable income.

PASS-THROUGH DEDUCTION

Owning real estate brings yet another valuable benefit: the pass-through deduction. If you operate your real estate business as a pass-through entity like a partnership, S corporation, or sole proprietorship, you may qualify for a significant tax deduction.

The pass-through deduction allows eligible businesses to deduct up to 20 percent of their qualified business income from their taxable income. If your real estate business generates $10,000 in qualified business income, you can deduct $2,000.

That covers all our deductions. Here's where we are so far:

Rental property cost	$300,000
Annual net rental income	$10,000
Operating expense deduction	$10,000
Mortgage interest deduction	$7,456
Depreciation deduction	$10,909
Owner expense deduction	$10,000
Pass-through deduction	$2,000
TOTAL DEDUCTIONS	**$40,365**

Who doesn't want $13,000 less in taxes? And we're not even done yet. There are still more tax cuts you can get from rental real estate investments.

OTHER TAX BENEFITS

There are several remaining tax advantages to rental real estate you should be aware of. One constitutes true tax savings, and the other two have to do with delaying or deferring deductions or taxes. Let's take a look.

AVOID FICA TAXES

Federal Insurance Contributions Act (FICA) taxes may not be the most enjoyable part of earning a paycheck, but they play a crucial role in funding Social Security and Medicare. The Social Security portion goes toward supporting retirement benefits, while the Medicare portion contributes to healthcare for seniors. You know Social Security can't really be counted on from earlier in this book, though, so paying these taxes in full may leave a bad taste in your mouth. That's where real estate comes to the rescue.

Real estate investments can help you avoid paying FICA taxes. When you earn income through rental properties, it falls under the category of passive income rather than earned income. And you'll be glad to know that passive income is not subject to FICA taxes.

So how much of a savings does this amount to? At the time of writing, FICA taxes total 7.65 percent of active earnings (6.2 percent for Social Security and 1.45 percent for Medicare). Assuming $10,000 in annual net rental income, that's a savings of $765.

COST SEGREGATION

Cost segregation for real estate investments can have a remarkable impact on your tax savings. It has to do with depreciation, which we talked about earlier in the context of your real estate investment. Through cost segregation, you can accelerate the depreciation deduction on certain other components of your property so you can save more now.

As the name suggests, cost segregation involves breaking down the costs associated with your property into various components, such as land, buildings, and specific improvements. By segregating the costs, you get to enjoy larger deductions during the early years of ownership. This is helpful if you just dumped a bunch of money into the investment and need to recoup some of the costs.

Here's how this might look for our fictional $300,000 rental property. Let's say that after conducting a cost segregation analysis, 25 percent of the property's value can be allocated to components eligible for accelerated depreciation. The segregated costs amount to $75,000.

Without cost segregation, the depreciation deduction would typically be spread over the standard 27.5-year period for residential rental properties. However, with cost segregation, you could accelerate the depreciation on the segregated portion, say, to a shorter depreciation period of fifteen years.

Yes, that's a lot, but stick with me for just a few more sentences. Using the straight-line depreciation method, the annual depreciation deduction for the segregated portion would be $5,000 ($75,000 divided by fifteen years). That means that over the first five years, the cumulative tax savings from accelerated depreciation through cost segregation could amount to approximately $25,000! That was worth the math, right?

DEFERRING CAPITAL GAINS TAX

Our last advantage of real estate investing is the ability to defer capital gains tax. I mentioned capital gains tax briefly in the tax chapter; it's a type of tax imposed on the profit earned from the sale or disposal of certain assets, such as stocks, real estate, or other investments. It is calculated based on the difference between the selling price and the original purchase price of the asset, and it can end up eating up a lot of your profit. Rates can vary depending on factors such as the holding period and your income level.

While deferring taxes isn't generally a good idea, as you already learned, it can help you if you're using the deferred taxes to help you make more money-making investments. Let's say you flip a property and generate a profit. Typically, you'd have to pay capital gains tax the next year. However, by reinvesting that profit into another qualifying property within a specific time frame, you can delay paying the capital gains tax and keep your money working for you. This powerful strategy is called a 1031 exchange, or a like-kind exchange.

Factoring in those additional tax benefits, here's where our hypothetical annual tax savings now stand:

Rental property cost	$300,000
Annual gross rental income	$24,000
Operating expense deduction	$12,000
Mortgage interest deduction	$8,000
Depreciation deduction	$10,909
Owner expense deduction	$10,000
Pass-through deduction	$1,536
FICA tax savings	$765
Cost segregation	$1,600
Deferred capital gains tax	N/A
TOTAL DEDUCTIONS	$42,730

A REAL SOLID INVESTMENT

You can probably tell that I'm a huge advocate of real estate investments, and I hope this chapter has helped you understand why. I own millions in real estate myself!

Real estate is incredibly difficult to surpass in terms of its potential. It provides safety, stability, and so many potential tax benefits. It's a cardinal example of good debt, providing an exceptional avenue for both short-term and long-term growth.

You can invest in real estate at any age, but your twenties through your fifties are a particularly great time to invest in real estate if you can afford it. While you've got the energy, you can manage the headaches of real estate ownership. Then, during retirement, you can then sell your real estate, cash out, and have a big lump sum of money to enjoy for the rest of your life. Alternatively, if you have the stomach for it, you can keep it and enjoy the income, and then pass on a tax-free benefit to your heirs. At the very least, invest in real estate by owning your own home and paying off that mortgage as soon as you can. Whether you're a private homeowner or a property mogul, though, there's no avoiding the power of real estate—even if it puts you in debt in the short term.

5

LONG-TERM CARE COVERAGE AT 50 PERCENT OFF

Writer and philanthropist Tia Walker wrote, "To care for those who once cared for us is one of the highest honors."[48] Long-term care is a great example of this, and it's extremely common. Seven out of ten people will find themselves in a long-term care situation before they pass,[49] so it is arrogant for us to assume we won't find ourselves in need of such care.

A long-term care situation involves a chronic illness that prevents you from performing two out of the six activities of daily living (ADLs) for a period exceeding ninety days. To clarify, the six ADLs are eating, bathing,

---

48   Peggi Speers and Tia Walker, *The Inspired Caregiver: Finding Joy While Caring for Those You Love* (North Charleston, SC: CreateSpace Independent Publishing Platform, 2013).

49   "How Much Care Will You Need?," US Department of Health and Human Services, updated February 18, 2020, https://acl.gov/ltc/basic-needs/how-much-care-will-you-need.

dressing, toileting, transferring, and continence.[50] This type of care is expensive, so long-term care coverage is a significant aspect of financial planning. It plays a crucial role in safeguarding your future, often marking the difference between a safe, comfortable living situation and a truly devastating catastrophe where you can't afford the care you need.

In this chapter, I'll help you navigate this sticky part of financial planning. I'll highlight some of the challenges associated with stand-alone long-term care coverage and present three innovative alternatives that provide comparable benefits at a fraction of the cost. But first, let's see what we're *really* up against.

DON'T LET LONG-TERM CARE DRAIN YOUR ESTATE

Long-term care is among the major bankruptcy factors in the United States. It's not covered by Medicare, Medicare Supplement plans, or Medicare Advantage plans. That means if you find yourself in a long-term care situation, meaning you are unable to perform two out of the six ADLs for a period exceeding ninety days, you will need to cover the expenses either with your own finances or with a long-term care insurance plan.

---

50 "Long Term Care Insurance," California Department of Insurance, revised January 2014, https://www.insurance.ca.gov/01-consumers/105-type/95-guides/05-health/01-ltc/ltc-insurance.cfm.

There is added strain here because people are living longer and longer, which means they're racking up larger and larger long-term care bills. There are a lot of reasons for our increased longevity, including improved nutrition and living conditions. The role of technology, particularly artificial intelligence (AI), also can't be ignored. There is a common debate on whether AI will lead to our destruction or extend our lifespan; some people even think AI will become sentient and kill us all! While this makes for dramatic Hollywood movies, AI is more likely to do the opposite for us. It has the potential to revolutionize the medical field and improve healthcare outcomes.

For instance, for every 100 MRI scans, there is often an anomaly that can be misdiagnosed.[51] AI technology can help identify and eliminate these anomalies, leading to more accurate diagnoses. This advancement in healthcare will contribute to longer human lifespans. Of course, that's a wonderful thing, but it will ultimately increase the cost of long-term care even more.

As of right now, in my home state of Tennessee, the average cost of long-term care is already $54,912.[52] If the stay is related to Alzheimer's or dementia, the average cost

---

51 Ross Hauser, "Is My MRI Accurate? Is It Reliable?," Caring Medical, updated July 22, 2022, https://www.caringmedical.com/prolotherapy-news/getting-accurate-mri/.

52 "Genworth Cost of Survey | Median Cost Data Tables," Genworth, January 31, 2022, https://pro.genworth.com/riiproweb/productinfo/pdf/282102.pdf

increases by as much as $1,000 per month,[53] resulting in a $66,912 sticker price.[54] By the time you need long-term care, it will likely be even higher. Is your plan set up to handle that kind of blow?

My extended family is all too aware of this problem. I have a relative named Michael who owned a very successful tile contracting business and was a millionaire. He had been married to his lovely wife, Jane, for three decades, and everything was going well. Then, in her late fifties, Jane started having symptoms that required long-term care. Jane's body was very strong and healthy, but her brain was struggling.

Unfortunately, Michael didn't have anything in place to help facilitate the cost of care, so he was forced to try to help her more and more himself. Over time, Jane's need for care increased so much that Michael was unable to continue his tile business. He had to shut it down, and after his income stream was removed, he had to start liquidating his retirement savings to help cover the ongoing cost of taking care of his wife.

Jane ended up lasting over twelve years in that situation. Because they did not have long-term care

---

53   Christine Lacagnina, "Tennessee Long Term Care Insurance," Trusted Choice, October 17, 2019, https://www.trustedchoice.com/long-term-care-insurance/state/tennessee/.

54   "Cost of Care Survey," Genworth, updated June 2, 2022, https://www.genworth.com/aging-and-you/finances/cost-of-care.html.

coverage, Michael had to liquidate essentially all of his assets. By the time Jane passed away, all Michael had left was the equity in his house, which he had to sell and move to a cheaper state because he had nothing left to live on. It's so sad because now he is dealing with Alzheimer's himself and he has no assets to support his care, so he has to rely on the Medicaid system. This is so unfortunate and tragic, considering Michael and Jane's original financial potential. Two long-term care situations, first with Michael's wife and now with Michael himself, completely depleted a seven-figure, hard-won fortune.

The good news is that some foresight can help you avoid this. Knowing that the vast majority of retirees will find themselves in need of long-term care and understanding what such a situation can do to your finances, it's crucial to get long-term care coverage to protect your assets. However, that opens up a whole new can of worms.

THREE BIG DRAWBACKS OF STAND-ALONE LONG-TERM CARE INSURANCE POLICIES

When you look at the history of stand-alone long-term care insurance, you'll find that the majority of long-term care companies have gone bankrupt. This is largely because healthcare is the only sector where technology does not make things more affordable; it actually makes things *more* expensive, as I outlined briefly in the last section.

Healthcare tech, while life-saving, is also exorbitantly expensive, and insurance companies vastly underestimated the ongoing increase in the cost of long-term care they would cover. Then, when they had to provide coverage for policies, they went under.[55]

Today, there are only a handful of long-term care companies left that offer stand-alone long-term care insurance policies. So should you snap one up? No. Aside from financial solvency, there are some big problems with stand-alone long-term care insurance policies you should be aware of as a buyer.

1. UNLIMITED PREMIUM INCREASES

First, your long-term care insurance premiums on stand-alone LTC policies can continue to increase throughout your life with no end in sight. Policies generally do not specify a maximum increase, and when you inquire about this, you'll get some kind of vague response. Even if you find a decent starting premium, those premiums can continue to rise throughout your lifetime, whether it's on an annual basis or every five years. This can land you with an enormous monthly bill you weren't expecting.

According to a recent report by the National Association of Insurance Commissioners (NAIC) Long-Term Care

---

55   Alexander Sammon, "The Collapse of Long-Term Care Insurance," The American Prospect, October 20, 2020, https://prospect.org/familycare/the-collapse-of-long-term-care-insurance/.

Insurance Task Force (2021), among a pool of 3,500 approved rate increases nationwide, the average single approved rate hike was 37 percent and the average cumulative approved rate increase was 112 percent. You read that right—112 percent! The average policyholder-attained age in the most rate-increased blocks was 74.8 years old, with a range of 72.7 to 76.8 years old. If you live into your eighties or nineties, it only gets worse.[56] Are you prepared to pay premiums like that?

2. NO BENEFIT UNLESS YOU GET SICK

Second, if you happen to be among the individuals who do not require long-term care coverage before they pass away,[57] there is no death benefit or return of premium. Essentially, all the premiums you have paid, often amounting to tens or even hundreds of thousands of dollars, do not provide any benefit upon your death. They go straight down the toilet. The insurance company keeps the money, and you receive nothing in return for tens if not hundreds of thousands in premiums spent.

56 Brenda J. Cude, Lisa Groshong, and Bonnie Burns, "Long-Term Care Insurance Rate Increases and Reduced Benefit Options: Insights from Interviews with Financial Planners," National Association of Insurance Commissioners (NAIC), Center for Insurance Policy and Research, November 2022, https://content.naic.org/sites/default/files/long-term-care-insurance-rate-increases-and-reduced-benefit-options-insights-from-interviews-with-financial-planners.pdf.

57 "How Much Care Will You Need?," 2020.

3. AN INEFFICIENT REIMBURSEMENT STYLE

The third problem with stand-alone long-term care insurance plans is that they follow a reimbursement style rather than covering costs up front. This means you have to personally pay for the services and care and then submit the receipts to the insurance company every month for reimbursement. The average time for reimbursement is between one and three months for most companies, and these are not small bills you're fronting. This process is cumbersome, tiresome, inefficient, and frustrating. Having to go back and forth every month to seek reimbursement can be a significant hassle and a pain in the butt, and this often has to be done by caregivers or relatives.

ALTERNATIVE OPTIONS TO LONG-TERM CARE COVERAGE

As you can see, there are expensive and just plain annoying aspects to stand-alone long-term care coverage. Luckily, there are three alternative options that are both innovative and more cost-effective than such a policy. Here are some great alternative options to traditional long-term care insurance. With living benefits through a life insurance product, the inclusion of long-term care doublers on annuities, and the availability of guaranteed issue long-term care lump sum products, you can avoid the massive expense and hassle of long-term care insurance and still get some peace of mind and protection for your estate.

LIVING BENEFITS THROUGH A LIFE INSURANCE PRODUCT

Usually, when I mention life insurance, people automatically think about death benefits. Death benefits are payouts that go to your family when you pass away, and they're the main reason people seek out life insurance. In this case, however, you are not purchasing a life insurance policy solely for the death benefit. These are life insurance policies that offer a feature called *living benefits*. These living benefits typically include three riders, and the good news is that these riders are often provided free of charge with your policy. Yes, as long as you have life insurance, you might get these benefits for *free*.

These three alternative methods for obtaining long-term care coverage are more cost-effective than a stand-alone policy as they can be acquired at a reduced cost of 25 to 50 percent compared to traditional long-term care options. However, there are a few important things to keep in mind.

- There may be a waiting period before the benefits can be accessed.

- This could affect your estate. Any amount received through the riders will be subtracted from the eventual benefit paid to the policyholder's beneficiaries, impacting the total payout.

- As with any life insurance policy, this type of coverage requires you to qualify for it based on your health. If you're already in poor shape, it may be an expensive option for you. However, if you're still relatively young and healthy, it's definitely worth a look.

Now, let's take a look at each of these riders and what kind of coverage they provide.

1. **Terminal Illness Rider.** The terminal illness rider allows you to accelerate and access a portion of the death benefit (or even the whole thing) tax-free while you are still alive. This rider comes into play if a doctor has informed you that you have less than a year to live. You can use this money for end-of-life care and related expenses, of course, but a lot of people also use it for fun stuff. You could, for example, use some of the funds to go on a fantastic vacation with your family.

2. **Chronic Illness Rider.** The second rider essentially covers long-term care situations. If

you are unable to perform two out of the six ADLs, you are considered to have a chronic illness, and this rider kicks in. You can then accelerate a portion, or in certain cases, the entire death benefit, while you are still alive, to cover the cost of care.

3. **Critical Illness Rider.** The critical illness rider provides benefits if you experience certain acute health issues like a heart attack, stroke, cancer, blindness, or loss of a limb. If you end up with any of these critical illnesses, you can accelerate a portion, or in specific circumstances, the entire death benefit, while you are still alive.

By incorporating these riders into your life insurance policy, you essentially gain long-term care benefits at a fraction of the cost compared to stand-alone long-term care plans. Think of it as a backdoor way for you to accomplish long-term care benefits for a fraction of the cost. The beautiful part is, this is also life insurance in the traditional sense. If you don't utilize the living benefits for terminal, chronic, or critical illness, your loved ones receive a tax-free death benefit. It's not a matter of *if* it pays, but rather *when* it pays. You're not losing any expensive premiums like you do with a normal stand-alone long-term care policy.

LONG-TERM CARE DOUBLER ON AN ANNUITY

A long-term care doubler offers another approach to addressing long-term care expenses without having to dip into your retirement savings. Let's say you invest some of your assets into an annuity that pays you $5,000 per month. If you find yourself in a long-term care situation before passing away and you have a long-term care doubler, the monthly payment doubles. Instead of receiving $5,000, you receive $10,000 per month for up to five years. Plus, the long-term care doubler is included in the annuity for *free*.

The long-term care doubler on an annuity only requires qualification based on your financial health. This means that even if you are already dealing with physical health issues, the annuity option can still be a viable choice for you. This can make long-term care doublers a great option if you're already into your later years or you have some health issues.

GUARANTEED ISSUE LONG-TERM CARE LUMP SUM PRODUCT

Finally, we have the guaranteed issue long-term care lump sum product. Despite the less-than-catchy name, this is a powerful product that can have an enormous impact on your care. You basically take a lump sum of money to buy permanent long-term care coverage. Because you pay in advance, you can't be blindsided by skyrocketing premiums—you know exactly how much is going in. For instance, you can take a lump sum, such as $100,000, and use it to purchase $250,000 worth of long-term care coverage.

Like the long-term care doubler, you can buy a guaranteed issue long-term care lump sum product regardless of how unhealthy you are. You can get your hands on this even if you are already in a long-term care situation and facing health challenges. Sure, $100,000 isn't exactly pocket change, but if you're in decent financial shape, it also won't drain your retirement fund or put you in bankruptcy. In many long-term care situations, the bill far exceeds $100,000, so the guaranteed issue long-term care lump sum product helps you navigate long-term care with minimal financial strain.

LONG-TERM CARE COVERAGE DONE RIGHT

I hope I've driven home the point that long-term care is a big deal. Protecting your estate from the potential financial drain of long-term care expenses is critical; failing to do so bankrupts many successful, smart people every year. Plus, as humans live longer, the costs associated with prolonged lifespans increase in kind. This means that expenses related to long-term care coverage will increase as well, and Medicaid may not be there to step in, so you should really take care of it as soon as you can.

Since stand-alone long-term care insurance policies are often less than ideal, with their unlimited premium increases and inefficient reimbursement styles, it's a good thing there are alternative options available. Living benefits through life insurance products, such as terminal illness, chronic illness, and critical illness riders; long-term care doublers on an annuity; and guaranteed issue long-term care lump sum products are all good options for protecting your estate and providing for yourself and your loved ones.

I found a solution for my long-term care in my thirties. Very few people do that, but you should do it as soon as possible because you never know what will happen. Life can really throw curveballs at you, and you never know when you'll need this kind of protection.

So, which long-term care option is best for you? It depends on your income plan, estate, health, and other factors. Don't forget to consult with a qualified financial professional to assess your specific situation and determine the best strategy for protecting your estate and securing your peace of mind. We offer a free fifteen-minute phone consultation to answer your specific questions about long-term care. You can simply go to www.retirementrenegade.com to request your free, no-obligation consultation so you can know how to set up your retirement with the best long-term care strategy for you!

6
SOLO SOCIAL SECURITY

Have you heard of ostrich syndrome? Ostriches live in desert regions and they lay their eggs underground for protection. Since they have very long necks, they are able to stand up while putting their head in their underground nests to rotate their eggs and make sure they are evenly heated in the desert climate. It looks comical, doesn't it? The popular myth holds that they could, if they felt like it, simply stick their heads in the sand to avoid thinking about or facing unpleasant realities. Chicks being annoying? Head in the sand. Time to clean up the nest? Head in the sand. Don't feel like hunting for lizards? Head in the sand. They don't actually do this, but ostrich syndrome definitely does exist in other species, if not in a literal sense.

To illustrate, let me give you a fact that, understandably, causes ostrich syndrome in a lot of my clients. Did you know that 80 percent of men are married when they pass away? And since men have shorter lifespans than women, unfortunately 80 percent of women die single.

Many of them face widowhood unprepared.[58] A big part of that is Social Security planning, and it all *really* comes down to this one key question: When should I claim my Social Security benefits?

Making the wrong call about when to take Social Security can significantly affect your retirement, especially for women. In fact, it is estimated that, depending on how long you live, making the wrong decision about claiming Social Security can cost you between $100,000 and $500,000 overall during your retirement.[59] Is that money *you* can afford to lose?

So is there a one-size-fits-all answer? Of course not. It depends on how much you earned during your working years, among other factors. However, I can say with confidence that panicking and sticking your head in the sand won't help. Ostriches don't actually stick their heads in the sand, and neither should you.

In this chapter, we will look at all things Social Security. First, we'll talk about why this is important even though Social Security is on unstable footing. Then we'll discuss how Social Security payouts work, factoring in

58　Alessandra Malito, "This is something young married women should pay attention to," MarketWatch, July 29, 2017, https://www.marketwatch.com/story/this-is-something-young-married-women-should-pay-attention-to-2017-04-28

59　Janna Herron, "Doing This One Thing with Your Social Security Could Mean Losing $100,000 in Retirement," USA TODAY, June 28, 2019, https://www.usatoday.com/story/money/2019/06/28/social-security-claim-too-early-and-lose-100-000-retirement/1572620001/.

elements like your full retirement age and deferred retirement credits. Next, we'll consider common life factors (like whether you're a breadwinner or a homemaker) and how these affect your retirement strategy. By considering the underlying math and understanding how they affect your income plan, you can make well-informed choices tailored to your specific needs instead of spur-of-the-moment choices based on fear. So pull your head out of the sand and let's take a closer look at Social Security.

GET IT WHILE THE GETTIN'S GOOD? SOCIAL SECURITY IN AN UNSTABLE TIME

"We have heard from the news and many trusted sources that Social Security is running out of money, so I better get it while the getting is good."

"I better turn it on as soon as I can."

"Maybe I should claim it as soon as possible, even at age sixty-two, just to secure some benefits."

People say this kind of stuff to me all the time about when the topic of Social Security comes up, and for good reason. Do you remember reading about Social Security in Chapter 1? In its current state—unless significant legislative action is taken—Social Security is heading toward a financial crisis. The government could run out of money for Social Security and may have to reduce its benefits by a third sooner than 2033, and it's advisable to plan for that.

However, just because Social Security will eventually face cuts doesn't mean you should prematurely activate your Social Security income. Sure, your car will eventually stop working, but that doesn't mean you should take it to the impound lot now!

A good financial advisor (and frankly, there aren't many these days) should be knowledgeable about Social Security's underfunded liabilities and help you create a Social Security stopgap fund like I mentioned in Chapter 1. To recap, this is a pool of money that you set aside for when Social Security is cut by a third. This fund, which has been safely growing, can be withdrawn or turned into some form of annuity to supplement your income when it is needed. This way, you won't experience a reduction in your monthly revenue or income if and when Social Security gets cut by a third.

If your advisor hasn't discussed this with you, you need to find a different advisor because this is a *very, very* important topic. At Retirement Renegade, we specialize in creating Social Security stopgap funds, so give us a call if you need help with this.

I also have to remind you here that your handling of Social Security depends a whole lot on that income plan you've hopefully crafted by now. An income plan that factors in all of your saved resources for retirement plays a vital role in when you should turn Social Security on. It is not just about waiting until full retirement age. You need to ask yourself, "What other assets do I have saved?" "When was I planning on retirement?" "How is my health?" "Am I stressed out of my mind at my current job?" All of that needs to be considered.

To do *any* effective financial planning, you need to create an income plan. That's the only way to ensure that you are making informed decisions regarding Social Security, which is one of the most crucial decisions you will make in retirement. It's also critical to have an advisor who can help you in navigating this important decision, since there are a lot of factors involved in when to take Social Security. This, in large part, lies in the way Social Security payouts work.

HOW SOCIAL SECURITY PAYOUTS WORK

Before I explain the optimal time to take Social Security, let me tell you a little bit about how Social Security works when it's time to cash in.

Everyone has a designated full retirement age (FRA) based on their birth year. If you were born in or before 1955, the FRA is set at sixty-six years and two months. This time span gradually increases to sixty-seven for those born in 1960 or later. You can check out a full chart at SSA.gov to figure out your exact FRA if you were born between 1956 and 1959.

Once you start receiving benefits, depending on which side of the FRA you retire on, your payments can vary a lot. Time to get into the weeds.

DELAYED RETIREMENT CREDITS

If you delay claiming benefits past your FRA, your monthly benefit increases. That's right—it literally pays to wait. By deferring your Social Security benefits, you earn delayed retirement credits. For each year you wait beyond your FRA, up until age 70, your benefit amount grows by approximately 8 percent per year. These credits accumulate until you reach the maximum credit at age seventy.

Let me put this in context for you. Let's say that Mary, an architect born in 1961, has reached her FRA of sixty-seven. She is now eligible to claim her Social Security benefits without a penalty, and her estimated monthly benefit at her FRA is $1,500. Mary, however, is feeling spry and loves her job too much to leave just yet. She decides to wait and delay her benefits for three additional years until age seventy.

For each year of delay, Mary earns delayed retirement credits, which increase her monthly benefit amount. Assuming an approximate 8 percent increase per year, Mary would receive a total increase of 24 percent (8 percent per year for three years) on top of her FRA benefit amount. That amounts to an extra $360 per month when she starts receiving Social Security benefits. Over the course of a year, Mary would receive an additional $4,320 by opting for the delayed retirement strategy!

EARLY RETIREMENT REDUCTION

So if you wait to receive benefits, you get a bonus. However, if you claim benefits before reaching your FRA, your monthly benefit amount is reduced.

Let's look at Mary's case again. We know Mary's FRA is sixty-seven, but in this scenario, at age sixty-four, she gets into a horrible argument with her boss. Fed up, she decides to quit her job and retire three years early.

When claiming benefits before reaching her FRA, Mary now faces an early retirement reduction. This reduction is calculated based on just how many months early Mary's payments begin. If you're curious, you can view a breakdown on SSA.gov.

The reduction for starting benefits three years early is approximately 20 percent. Therefore, by claiming her benefits at age sixty-four instead of waiting until her FRA, Mary's monthly benefit would be reduced by $300. She would therefore only receive $1,200 per month instead of the full benefit amount. Over the course of a year, this means Mary would lose out on $3,600 ($300 x 12 months) in Social Security benefits.

Here's a full breakdown of how Mary's Social Security start date could affect her payouts:

SCENARIO	MARY'S CLAIMING AGE	MARY'S FRA	MONTHLY BENEFIT	YEARLY BENEFIT
Delayed Benefits	Age 70	67	$1,860	$22,320
FRA Benefits	Age 67	67	$1,500	$18,000
Early Benefits	Age 64	67	$1,200	$14,400

LONGEVITY

There's one more factor you need to consider here: time. Time comes for us all, but it's also unpredictable as to when exactly that will expire. At the time of writing, the average lifespan is around eighty-seven for women and eighty-four for men.

This next table shows what Mary's total SS benefits will look like if she lives to be a variety of different ages. She could live to be seventy-five (if she were to get sick or be involved in an accident); eighty-four; eighty-seven (the average); ninety; or a full 100 years. This chart contains figures for Mary if she lived to those ages and retired at the three different retirement ages described in the last section. As you can see, this is where things get kind of complicated, and this chart doesn't even factor in inflation.

LIFESPAN	DELAYED BENEFITS (AGE 70): $22,320/YEAR	FRA BENEFITS (AGE 67): $18,000/YEAR	EARLY BENEFITS (AGE 64): $14,400/YEAR
To Age 75	$111,600	$126,000	$162,000
To Age 84	$312,480	$306,000	$288,000
To Age 87	$379,000	$360,000	$331,200
To Age 90	$446,400	$414,000	$374,400
To Age 100	$669,600	$594,000	$518,400

First, check out 100-year-old Mary's payout numbers. By delaying benefits until age 70, she increased her overall benefits by over $75,000 compared to if she had retired at her FRA! However, if Mary gets sick and dies at 75, it would have been better for her to have taken those early benefits. You can see clearly that it's all about playing the numbers game depending on your situation.

SPOUSAL BENEFITS AND SURVIVOR BENEFITS

In the examples from the last section, no mention is made of Mary's spouse. If you are married, whether you're the primary breadwinner, a secondary earner, or a homemaker, there are two extra Social Security concepts you should be aware of before it's time to take a look at some specific scenarios.

SPOUSAL BENEFITS

If you were a stay-at-home parent and raised your children for many years, you may have fewer Social Security credits, resulting in a smaller monthly benefit. In that case, you may be eligible to receive half the amount of your husband's Social Security if his benefit is higher than yours. Here's the cool part: Claiming a spousal benefit does not reduce the eligible spouse's own benefit! The spousal benefit is separate and does not impact the primary earner's benefit amount. So your husband will still get his full benefit even if you end up qualifying for the spousal benefit.

To be eligible for a spousal benefit, you have to meet three criteria:

1. The spouse seeking the benefit must be at least sixty-two years old.

2. The other spouse must already be receiving their own Social Security retirement or disability benefit.

3. The couple must have been married for at least one year.[60]

Also, keep in mind that a spousal benefit may result in a reduction if the spouse starts receiving benefits before their full retirement age. The actual amount received as a spousal benefit depends on factors like how old you are, the primary earner's benefit amount, and the timing of the claim. There are specific parameters around this, so remember to seek personal advice from a qualified and capable advisor who specializes in Social Security.

SURVIVOR BENEFITS

Survivor benefits kick in when someone who has worked and paid into Social Security dies. At that point, their surviving spouse or other eligible family members can get some of their Social Security benefits. The idea is to help out the surviving spouse and make sure they don't end up struggling financially after losing their spouse.

The survivor benefit amount depends on things like the deceased person's earnings history and when the surviving spouse starts collecting. However, they can be pretty generous. The surviving spouse can receive up to 100

---

60   "What Are the Marriage Requirements to Receive Social Security Spouse's Benefits? FAQ | SSA," Social Security Administration, last modified October 7, 2022, https://faq.ssa.gov/en-us/Topic/article/KA-01999.

percent of what the deceased spouse was getting from Social Security. That said, if the surviving spouse decides to claim the benefits before their FRA, the amount can go down just like it does for an individual's own Social Security.

Survivor benefits are especially important for secondary earners or homemakers. If you stayed home to take care of the kids, a survivor benefit can give you some income to cover your expenses and make things a bit easier if the worst should happen.

THE BEST TIME TO TURN ON SOCIAL SECURITY FOR YOUR SITUATION

Now that you understand a little more about how Social Security works, let's address three common scenarios that play a big role in when to take Social Security. Keep in mind that there is still other stuff you need to think about, like your income plan and assets. However, these three scenarios do tend to factor largely into people's decisions on when to cash in with the government.

YOU'RE THE PRIMARY BREADWINNER

If you are the primary breadwinner (or were during your working years), the question of when to take Social Security is especially important because it's not just about you. Others are counting on you as well, and you want to protect them. That's why, if you're the primary breadwinner, I highly recommend deferring Social Security until at least full retirement age.

As you discovered in the last section, Social Security is all a numbers game. In general, if you expect to live past age seventy-nine, it is beneficial for you to defer your retirement until you hit that FRA. You or your surviving family could receive tens or even hundreds of thousands of dollars more in Social Security benefits if you play your cards right, so this is the current recommendation as of the writing of this book, compared to claiming it at age sixty-two or even sixty-five.[61] Basically, if you do not have a chronic illness or are not struggling with a terminal condition, such as cancer, it is advantageous to defer your Social Security benefits. Just look at Mary's second chart again—the proof is in the numbers.

YOU'RE A HOMEMAKER OR A SECONDARY EARNER

If your spouse earned more during their working years, it may be acceptable for you to activate your Social Security benefits early. However, it would be advisable for *your spouse* to defer until full retirement age in this case. This is because if your spouse were to pass away, you would lose your smaller Social Security benefit but inherit their larger one, which you would enjoy for the rest of your life. This

---

61   David Altig, Laurence J. Kotlikoff, and Victor Yifan Ye. 2022. "How Much Lifetime Social Security Benefits Are Americans Leaving on the Table?," NBER Chapters, in: *Tax Policy and the Economy* 37:135-173.

rollover is called survivor benefits, and considering that four out of five men die while married[62] and four out of five women die single,[63] this is a real possibility for many married women.

Let's take a look at a real-world example of this. Imagine that lifelong homemaker Casey and her medical technician husband, David, are approaching retirement. Casey decides to activate her Social Security benefits early to supplement their income, but David decides to wait to activate his. Then, David gets into a car accident one evening on the way home from work and tragically passes away. Casey, who has activated her benefits early, loses her smaller benefit. However, she inherits David's larger benefit as a survivor benefit. This provides her with a more substantial and reliable source of income for the rest of her life.

Now, let's examine a scenario where David had decided to start taking Social Security before the accident. Since David opted to take Social Security early, his benefit amount was reduced. As a result, Casey is left with a reduced survivor benefit, which becomes her primary

---

62 Maya Dillon, "UBS Reveals Top Reason Married Women Step Aside in Long-Term Financial Decisions: They Believe Their Husbands Know More," UBS Wealth Management, May 14, 2018, https://www.ubs.com/global/de/media/display-page-ndp/en-20180514-ubs-reveals-top-reason.html.

63 Malito, "This is something young married women should pay attention to," 2017.

source of income after David's death. The reduced benefit amount puts a financial strain on Casey, making it more challenging for her to cover her expenses and maintain the same standard of living. She ends up having to downgrade to a smaller home and cut out vacations, restaurant meals, and visits to her beloved grandchildren.

You don't want to end up in that situation! Opting to delay taking benefits can ensure a higher survivor benefit for the spouse left behind, providing greater financial stability and support during a difficult time. That's why it is very important for a spouse who is the primary bread-winner, if they aren't sick or in really bad health, to defer until at least full retirement age, even if the other spouse takes their Social Security now.

YOU HAVE A CHRONIC ILLNESS

Now, let's take a look at a situation that requires the opposite advice. Remember Mary's Social Security payout result for the scenario where she lived to be seventy-five? What would she have done differently if she had *known* she'd die prematurely? She probably would have taken that early retirement.

If you're managing a chronic illness or you have a shorter life expectancy compared to the average person, it might make sense to start getting those Social Security benefits at your full retirement age or even earlier. That way, you'll have the financial support you need when times get tough.

If you have a chronic illness and can't work anymore because of your condition, it's time to activate your Social Security benefits.

Of course, everyone's situation is different, and there are other factors to consider when it comes to activating Social Security benefits. As a successful architect, Mary may have been able to fund that Dubai vacation even without Social Security. But if you don't have those financial safety nets, or even if you simply want to capitalize on those benefits, it's best to get the ball rolling as soon as possible.

CONDUCTOR OF THE SOCIAL SECURITY SYMPHONY

Have you ever gone to an orchestral concert? The conductor is in full control of the orchestra, slowing or speeding up the tempo, helping instrumental sections enter or exit the fray, and providing feeling and energy to the whole massive thing. When it comes to your Social Security benefits, you have that baton. You have the power to harmonize the different aspects of your Social Security benefits, creating an organized, swelling future that's filled with financial security.

We may not be able to count on Social Security not reducing benefits by a third, but that doesn't mean you shouldn't strategize. It's better to receive two-thirds of a higher payout for life than to receive two-thirds of a lower payout because of bad planning. By understanding the basics of Social Security payouts, such as delayed retirement credits and early retirement reduction, you can make informed decisions that match the tempo of your retirement plan. Remember to factor in dynamics like longevity, your financial role in your household, and spousal benefits.

If your financial advisor seems to gloss over this topic, or if you're not working with a financial professional, you need to find somebody who specializes in Social Security. At our firm, we specialize in Social Security and can guide you in making these important decisions regarding when to activate your income. Remember—with the right Social Security approach, you can orchestrate a fantastic, secure, and fun retirement.

7

THE RICHEST PLACE
ON EARTH

*"The wealthiest place on this planet is not the gold
mines, diamond mines, oil wells, or silver mines of
the earth, but the cemetery. Why? Because buried
in the graveyard are dreams and visions that were
never fulfilled, books that were never written,
paintings that were never painted, songs that were
never sang, and ideas that died as ideas."*[64]

— DR. MYLES MUNROE

Dr. Myles Munroe, a Bahamian evangelist and ordained
minister, famously used this quote to remind his congre-
gation of their potential. Within the cemetery, untapped
potential lies dormant. It's where paintings that were
never painted lie, where songs that were never sung reside,

---

64   Myles Munroe and T.D. Jakes, *Myles Munroe Devotional & Journal: 365
      Days to Realize Your Potential* (Shippensburg, PA: Destiny Image, 2007).

where businesses that were never started are buried deep in the ground, and where groundbreaking innovations that were never brought to fruition stay untapped forever. It's a resting place for unspoken sermons and ideas that were never manifested.

The richest place on Earth is the cemetery, as this is where human potential remains buried, unrealized by its intended originator. So, in this last chapter, I want to go in an unconventional direction and help you explore how financial freedom can help you release all that untapped potential.

FINANCIAL FEAR HOLDS YOU BACK

I believe we were put here on Earth for a reason. There is something unique about you, something special that only you can give. You were destined to do something. You have a very unique and specific assignment, a calling that I believe God has given to you. Are you fulfilling it right now? If you're like most people, you aren't. You've settled, and you're spending your precious time and resources doing something else.

I was lucky to discover my assignment early on. I wanted to help as many people as possible achieve financial freedom so they could enjoy their retirement and reach their potential. Thanks to my mom, I especially wanted to help women accomplish this. So in 2015, I started Legacy

Builders Wealth Management (now Retirement Renegade) with a clear goal: Prioritize the clients and address the needs of retirees and pre-retirees by offering guaranteed and secure retirement products.

The response was overwhelming, and in just seven months, our company's value soared to over $20 million. We had 200 agents across the nation assisting clients with their insurance and financial needs. None of that would have happened if I had let fear hold me back! Every day, I get to wake up and change people's lives, and there's nothing more rewarding than that.

Sadly, this isn't the usual story. All the time, we see countless ideas, inventions, and dreams that were never fulfilled, all tragically buried with the person who held them. Why does this happen? Why is it that all of this potential that we could and should have fulfilled in our lifetime ends up going to the grave with us? I believe it can be attributed to one primary reason: fear.

Too many times, I have witnessed people stop in their tracks because of fear. They don't take risks. They don't take a leap of faith. And often, that fear is *financial fear*. They tell me, "Well, Andrew, you know, I need to go to work. I need to provide and make sure I have enough money in retirement." Or, they say, "You know, the market goes up and down, and the market's down right now. There's no way I can step away from my job and pursue this business or idea I always have wanted to pursue. There's no way I can take time away from a busy schedule and focus on what I feel like God is calling me to."

WOMEN AND FINANCIAL FEAR

The data backs this up. According to a Pew Research study on how Americans view their jobs, among adults younger than thirty, only 44 percent report being extremely or very satisfied with their job overall. Workers aged sixty-five and older fare slightly better at 67 percent, but those folks will soon be leaving those fulfilling jobs. To make matters even worse for younger women, according to the study, women are more likely to find their job stressful and over-whelming.[65] How many of them are forced to stay in their difficult, taxing jobs because of financial fear?

Unfortunately, despite their job dissatisfaction, women may find it especially hard to overcome financial fear. A 2009 study conducted by the Kellogg School of Management at Northwestern University, the University of Chicago Booth School of Business, and the University of Chicago's Department of Comparative Human Development suggests that higher levels of testosterone in women are associated with a greater appetite for financial

---

65   Juliana Menasce Horowitz and Kim Parker, "How Americans View Their Jobs," Pew Research Center, March 30, 2023, https://www. pewresearch.org/social-trends/2023/03/30/how-americans-view-their-jobs/.

risk, which in turn affects their career decisions. Women with high levels of testosterone and low risk aversion, for example, are more likely to choose riskier careers in finance, which, at the time of this writing, is one example of a lucrative, male-dominated career.[66] According to the study, this can partially explain the wage gap and why women seem to constantly get the short end of the stick. But even if you're not a woman who likes living on the edge, it doesn't mean you can't overcome this fear.

TAPPING YOUR POTENTIAL

What if there was a way for your financial fear to be *settled* and to be dealt with so you could obtain that security, peace of mind, and protection of principal? You could then be able to pursue the dreams, desires, and potential that God put into your heart. This is why it is so important to have a financial plan that deals with and ultimately *eradicates* the financial fear. I believe that if your financial fear can be ultimately destroyed and dealt with, then you will have the freedom and room to pursue your potential.

No, money doesn't solve every problem, but there is a crucial link between financial stability and the ability to pursue one's calling. When you have a solid financial

66   "Study Shows Link between Testosterone and Women's Choice to Enter Finance Careers," *UChicago News*, August 25, 2009, https://news.uchicago.edu/story/study-shows-link-between-testosterone-and-womens-choice-enter-finance-careers.

foundation, you can dedicate your time, energy, and resources to your true purpose, as you were meant to.

TAPPING POTENTIAL BY SWITCHING CAREERS

As an example, let's take a look at Clara, a CPA and single mother with two college-age children. Clara is a talented writer, and she has a deep desire to write novels and share her stories with the world. She has been a successful CPA for decades. Her children both received generous financial aid packages from their respective universities, so she has the financial means to take time off work and pursue her passion. However, Clara is plagued by self-doubt and fear of failure. She constantly worries about the financial risks involved and whether her writing would be successful enough to sustain her, especially as she nears retirement. She talks to her family and friends, all of whom have traditional jobs and advise her not to rock the boat.

So Clara continues to put her dreams on hold and settles for her comfortable but unfulfilling career. Then, one day, she seeks the guidance of a financial planner who specializes in guaranteed increasing income for life (like me and our team at Retirement Renegade) to help her map out her retirement. Her intention was simply to cross her t's and dot her i's, but this financial planner does so much more than that. When Clara mentions in passing that she wants to be a writer, the financial planner helps Clara create a financial plan that includes converting the money she has saved into a guaranteed increasing income stream that covers all of her current bills plus extra each month for fun and traveling. Clara discovers that she can actually retire years earlier than she originally thought because she enough saved to secure her stepping away from her safe job and financially pursuing her dreams. This advisor came up with a full-spectrum retirement plan that factors in the best time to turn on Social Security, an estate plan, a tax plan to pay as little in taxes as possible, a LTC strategy, Medicare optimization, and a Social Security stopgap fund. Clara has a newfound hope. Clara has excitement! And for the first time in a long time, Clara is dreaming again.

With a clear plan in place from this unique, unconventional advisor, Clara implements the bulletproof retirement plan and immediately gains the confidence to pursue her writing full time. Ultimately, she finds a publisher for her novel and is even able to go on a small book tour and sign a contract for more books. When people tell her how much her books have touched their lives, she knows deep down that she has fulfilled her purpose.

ROB YOUR OWN GRAVE

Like Clara, we should be living in such a way that we want to rob the grave of its riches. We should strive to live up to our *full* potential, fulfilling all our assignments and destinies here on Earth, so that in the end, we can die empty. Yes—we want to go to the grave empty. We don't want to go to the grave full of untapped potential; instead, we want to leave everything here on Earth for others to enjoy and benefit from.

I can't help you discover your potential or destiny; there are plenty of other books for that. But if you KNOW in your heart where your true potential lies—or if you simply know that your current path will leave all your potential in that cemetery—proper financial planning with guarantees can free you to finally pursue that potential.

CONCLUSION: DON'T WAIT UNTIL IT'S TOO LATE

I hope you've gained some valuable insights about your safe retirement from this book, but none of what you've learned matters if you fail to act on it! Folks, life is too short to procrastinate. There is an old saying that comes to mind: "The best time to plant a tree was twenty years ago, and the second best time is today." People tend to procrastinate on these matters because they lack understanding. It feels as challenging as pulling teeth or hearing nails on a chalkboard to them. It's not enjoyable or exciting. They do not understand it. They feel embarrassed. They feel like they are going to make a foolish decision. So they put it off and neglect something as crucial as securing their financial future.

An interesting 2019 study showed that people spend more time daydreaming about their vacations each year than they do actually enjoying the vacation.[67] These people think, "Where should we go on vacation this year?" and spend all these hours doing research on the kind of vacation they want. They ponder questions like "Should we stay at that bungalow or head over to Bora Bora?" "Is there an all-you-can-eat or all-you-can-drink package?" "Are there any fun excursions we could try?" They invest so much time in studying, planning, and being intentional about their vacation. In the end, they devote more time to planning their one- or two-week vacation than they do to planning their 1,500-week vacation—their retirement!

On average, people will be retired for approximately *eighteen years*. That breaks down to 936 weeks. And if you happen to be among the one in five who lives longer, you would be retired for just over *twenty-eight years*, which translates to 1,500 weeks.[68] So if these people were to spend even a fraction of the time they spend daydreaming about their one- to two-week vacation on planning for their 1,500-week retirement, or even a 936-week retirement, they would enjoy a retirement that lasts the rest of their lives.

---

67   Laurie Baratti, "New Study Shows How Often Americans Spend Daydreaming About Vacations," Travelpulse, October 27, 2019, https://www.travelpulse.com/news/features/new-study-shows-how-often-americans-spend-daydreaming-about-vacations.

68   Selena Maranjian, "Here's the Average Length of Retirement. Will Your Money Last That Long?," The Motley Fool, February 24, 2018, https://www.fool.com/retirement/2018/02/24/heres-the-average-length-of-retirement-will-your-m.aspx.

After planning for retirement, these people can daydream about their vacations. They can decide which island to go to, which bungalow to stay in, and how many tropical cocktails they'll enjoy with their loved ones or friends. They could truly be able to enjoy life to the fullest, right? They could figure out the number of trips they want to go on or missions they want to complete. They can create cherished memories, like taking their grandbabies to Disney World. They would be able to enjoy all these wonderful experiences if they would just spend a little time planning for their retirement.

So, my encouragement is this: Don't procrastinate! Don't bury your head in the sand and assume everything will magically be okay. Don't get sidetracked or over-whelmed by work or life's challenges. Making financial preparations for your future needs to be a priority. Remember: You always make time for what truly matters to you. If securing your financial future is a priority to you, you'll find a way to set some time aside for it. You will always make time for your priorities!

If you're still tempted to procrastinate, know this: Planning for retirement is actually a lot easier than people think. Many times, when individuals come into my office, they're surprised by how straightforward and painless the process is compared to how they thought it would go. It wasn't as bad as they imagined; in fact, for many of my clients, it's completely painless. But you have to take that first step! And I urge you not to procrastinate. Whether you feel like you haven't saved enough, you are content with your current situation, or you worry about the trajectory of your retirement, it is essential to get a second opinion.

Nobody is going to do this for you if you don't make a move. It's very important to get an income plan. It's very important to get a Social Security stopgap analysis. It's very important to go over your taxes and get a tax report done. It's very important to have a solid estate plan created, regardless of how much you have saved. It's really important to optimize your Medicare options for retirement. Retirement Renegade specializes in all of that, but we specialize by leading with safety. We take care of all the other things necessary for your retirement, of course, but our primary focus is on prioritizing *safety*.

In Chapter 1, you learned that income is queen. Having a steady income during retirement is like having a crown that keeps you financially empowered, and you have to get that in place.

In Chapter 2, you learned that getting rid of unnecessary risks is crucial in securing your hard-earned money. Wouldn't it be nice to enjoy restful nights without the worry of financial disaster lurking around the corner?

In Chapter 3, we delved into some IRS territory. Understanding the tax implications of retirement strategies can save you a boatload of money, and going over your taxes and getting a tax report done is crucial to that.

Then, in Chapter 4, we discussed some fantastic tax benefits and solid investment opportunities waiting for you in real estate. Are you set up to take advantage of all that?

Chapter 5 taught us how to protect ourselves from devastating long-term care with alternatives to stand-alone long-term care insurance and optimizing Medicare options.

In Chapter 6, we covered Social Security and when to start collecting benefits. Do you feel like that's a decision you are ready to make on your own?

Finally, in Chapter 7, we brought it all together. You are here for a reason, and financial freedom can go a long way toward helping you rise to your true potential. Especially as you approach retirement, it becomes less about "how much do you earn?" and more about "how much do you not lose?" That's the most important aspect.

Let me help you eliminate that financial fear and set you on a path to where your retirement *is* the vacation of your dreams. On this path, your entire future is bright and filled with happiness, knowing you'll be financially secure during your retirement. You have nothing but hope, joy, peace, fulfillment, and happiness to look forward to. However, you *need* to take the first step. You have to reach out to us.

Check out our website at retirementrenegade.com, and schedule an appointment. Even if it is a fifteen-minute phone call to start that conversation, you won't regret it. We have numerous resources available for you. You deserve to have the retirement you've always dreamed of, but remember, no one else can do it for you. You have to take the next step.

I hope you will. We look forward to speaking with you soon.

BIBLIOGRAPHY

"10 Things You Should Know About Bear Markets."
Hartford Funds. Accessed April 20, 2023. https://
www.hartfordfunds.com/practice-management/client-
conversations/managing-volatility/bear-markets.html.

ABC News. "The Pros and Many Cons of Variable
Annuities." *ABC News*, August 25, 2015. https://
abcnews.go.com/Business/pros-cons-variable-annuities/
story?id=33229630.

"Analysis of the Tax Cuts and Jobs Act," Tax
Policy Center. Accessed September 12, 2023.
https://www.taxpolicycenter.org/feature/
analysis-tax-cuts-and-jobs-act.

Altig, David, Laurence J. Kotlikoff, and Victor Yifan Ye. "How
Much Lifetime Social Security Benefits Are Americans
Leaving on the Table?" Kotlikoff, November 16, 2022.
https://kotlikoff.net/wp-content/uploads/2022/11/
How-Much-Lifetime-Social-Security-Benefits-Are-
Americans-Leaving-on-the-Table-11-16-22.pdf.

Baratti, Laurie. "New Study Shows How Often Americans Spend Daydreaming about Vacations." Travelpulse, October 27, 2019. https://www.travelpulse.com/news/features/new-study-shows-how-often-americans-spend-daydreaming-about-vacations.

Benna, Ted. *401k – Forty Years Later*. Maitland, FL: Xulon, 2018.

Bernard, Tara Siegel. "Variable Annuity Plus Guaranteed Income Merits Careful Scrutiny." *The New York Times*, June 19, 2015. https://www.nytimes.com/2015/06/20/your-money/variable-annuities-with-guaranteed-income-riders-require-careful-scrutiny.html.

Blue, Daniel. "Understanding Hidden Retirement Account Fees." *Forbes*, February 8, 2021. https://www.forbes.com/sites/forbesfinancecouncil/2021/02/08/understanding-hidden-retirement-account-fees.

Cohen, Patricia. "What Could Raising Taxes on the 1% Do? Surprising Amounts." *New York Times*, June 8, 2021. https://www.nytimes.com/2015/10/17/business/putting-numbers-to-a-tax-increase-for-the-rich.html.

"Consumer Expenditures Report 2019: BLS Reports." U.S. Bureau of Labor Statistics, December 22, 2020. https://www.bls.gov/opub/reports/consumer-expenditures/2019/home.htm.

"Cost of Care Survey." Genworth, updated June 2, 2022. https://www.genworth.com/aging-and-you/finances/cost-of-care.html.

Coumanakos, Ephie. "SECURE Act Basics: What Everyone Should Know." *Kiplinger*, March 24, 2020. https://www. kiplinger.com/article/retirement/t037-c032-s014-secure-act-basics-what-everyone-should-know.html.

"Countries with the Oldest Populations in the World." Population Reference Bureau. Accessed September 12, 2023. https://www.prb.org/resources/ countries-with-the-oldest-populations-in-the-world/

Coxwell, Kathleen. "TCJA and 2026 Tax Brackets: Why Your Taxes Are Likely to Increase and What to Do About It." NewRetirement, June 30, 2022. https://www.newretirement.com/ retirement/2026-tax-brackets-tcja-expiration/.

Cude, Brenda J., Lisa Groshong, and Bonnie Burns. "Long-Term Care Insurance Rate Increases and Reduced Benefit Options: Insights from Interviews with Financial Planners." National Association of Insurance Commissioners (NAIC), Center for Insurance Policy and Research, November 2022. https://content.naic.org/sites/ default/files/long-term-care-insurance-rate-increases-and-reduced-benefit-options-insights-from-interviews-with-financial-planners.pdf.

Dillon, Maya. "UBS Reveals Top Reason Married Women Step Aside in Long-Term Financial Decisions: They Believe Their Husbands Know More." UBS Wealth Management, May 14, 2018. https://www.ubs.com/ global/de/media/display-page-ndp/en-20180514-ubs-reveals-top-reason.html.

Euronews and AFP. "The Countries Where Population Is Declining." *Euronews*, January 20, 2023. https://www.euronews.com/2023/01/17/the-countries-where-population-is-declining.

Feather, William. *The Business of Life*. New York: Simon and Schuster, 1949.

Federal Deposit Insurance Corporation (FDIC). *Crisis and Response: An FDIC History, 2008-2013*. Washington, DC: FDIC, 2017.

Federal Trade Commission (FTC). *Federal Trade Commission Decisions: Volume 105*. Washington, DC: FTC, 1986.

Felix, Benjamin. "EPISODE 89: Wade PFAU: Safety-First: A Sensible Approach to Retirement Income Planning." *Rational Reminder*. March 12, 2020.

"Fiscal Data Explains the National Debt." Bureau of Fiscal Service, US Department of the Treasury, n.d. https://fiscaldata.treasury.gov/americas-finance-guide/national-debt/.

Franklin, Benjamin. *The Private Correspondence of Benjamin Franklin*, 2nd ed., vol. 1, edited by William Temple Franklin. London: Henry Colburn, 1817. https://babel.hathitrust.org/cgi/pt?id=umn.31951002057116d&view=1up&seq=296.

"Genworth Cost of Survey | Median Cost Data Tables," Genworth, January 31, 2022. https://pro.genworth.com/riiproweb/productinfo/pdf/282102.pdf.

Greenberg, Gregg. "Record demand for RILAs pushes Q3 annuity sales to new heights," *Investment News*, October 25, 2023, https://www.investmentnews.com/record-demand-for-rilas-pushes-q3-annuity-sales-to-new-heights-244864.

Greene, David. "Why Real Estate Builds Wealth More Consistently Than Other Asset Classes." *Forbes*, November 27, 2018. https://www.forbes.com/sites/davidgreene/2018/11/27/why-real-estate-builds-wealth-more-consistently-than-other-asset-classes/?sh=896d17054056.

Greene, Mark Richard. "Insurance: Definition, History, Types, Companies, & Facts." Encyclopedia Britannica. Updated November 16, 2023. https://www.britannica.com/topic/insurance/Historical-development-of-insurance.

Haskins, Justin. "IRS Data Proves Trump Tax Cuts Benefited Middle, Working-Class Americans Most." The Hill, December 4, 2021. https://thehill.com/opinion/finance/584190-irs-data-prove-trump-tax-cuts-benefited-middle-working-class-americans-most/.

Hauser, Ross. "Is My MRI Accurate? Is It Reliable?" Caring Medical, updated July 22, 2022. https://www.caringmedical.com/prolotherapy-news/getting-accurate-mri/.

Herron, Janna. "Doing This One Thing with Your Social Security Could Mean Losing $100,000 in Retirement." USA TODAY, June 28, 2019. https://www.usatoday.com/story/money/2019/06/28/social-security-claim-too-early-and-lose-100-000-retirement/1572620001/.

Horowitz, Juliana Menasce, and Kim Parker. "How Americans View Their Jobs." Pew Research Center, March 30, 2023. https://www. pewresearch.org/social-trends/2023/03/30/ how-americans-view-their-jobs/.

Horsley, Scott. "Social Security Is Now Expected to Run Short of Cash by 2033." NPR, March 31, 2023. https://www.npr.org/2023/03/31/1167378958/ social-security-medicare-entitlement-programs-budget.

"How Much Care Will You Need?" US Department of Health and Human Services, updated Accessed November 21, 2023. https://acl.gov/ltc/basic-needs/ how-much-care-will-you-need.

"How Will Boomers Affect Social Security?" National Academy of Social Insurance. https://www.nasi.org/learn/social-security/ how-will-boomers-affect-social-security/.

"Human Rights." *Firing Line* broadcast records, March 9, 1977. Hoover Institution Library & Archives. https:// digitalcollections.hoover.org/objects/6450/human-rights.

Iacurci, Greg. "Secure 2.0 Changes 3 Key Rules Around Required Withdrawals from Retirement Accounts." CNBC, January 3, 2023. https://www.cnbc. com/2023/01/03/3-changes-in-secure-2point0-for-required-minimum-distributions.html.

"Invest Your Money in Land," *Pearson's Magazine*. United States: Pearson Publishing Company, Volume 26, 1911.

Issa, Erin El. "Financial Fees Could Cost Americans $1.1 Million Over Their Lifetime." NerdWallet, updated August 7, 2018. https://www.nerdwallet.com/article/investing/financial-fees-study-2018.

Kotowska, Irena E, et. al. "Second European Quality of Life Survey: Family Life and Work." European Commission, 2010. Reprinted in Ideas, *Time* online, May 2012. https://ideas.time.com/wp-content/uploads/sites/5/2012/02/efl002en.pdf.

Lacagnina Christine. "Tennessee Long Term Care Insurance," Trusted Choice. October 17, 2019, https://www.trustedchoice.com/long-term-care-insurance/state/tennessee/.

"LIMRA: 2022 U.S. Retail Annuity Sales Shatter Annual Sales Records Set in 2008." LIMRA, January 26, 2023. https://www.limra.com/en/newsroom/news-releases/2023/limra-2022-u.s.-retail-annuity-sales-shatter-annual-sales-records-set-in-2008/.

Lite, Jordan. "Death on Mount Everest: The Perils of the Descent." Scientific American Blog Network, December 10, 2008. https://blogs.scientificamerican.com/news-blog/death-on-mount-everest-the-perils-o-2008-12-10/.

"Long Term Care Insurance." California Department of Insurance, revised January 2014. https://www.insurance.ca.gov/01-consumers/105-type/95-guides/05-health/01-ltc/ltc-insurance.cfm.

Malito, Alessandra. "This is something young married women should pay attention to." MarketWatch, July 29, 2017. https://www.marketwatch.com/story/this-is-something-young-married-women-should-pay-attention-to-2017-04-28.

Maranjian, Selena. "Here's the Average Length of Retirement. Will Your Money Last That Long?" The Motley Fool, February 24, 2018. https://www.fool.com/retirement/2018/02/24/heres-the-average-length-of-retirement-will-your-m.aspx.

Munnell, Alicia H., Wenliang Hou, and Geoffrey T. Sanzenbacher. 2018. *National Retirement Risk Index Shows Modest Improvement in 2016.* Center for Retirement Research Issue Brief 18-1. January 2018. https://crr.bc.edu/wp-content/uploads/2018/01/IB_18-1.pdf.

Munroe, Myles. *Rediscovering the Kingdom: Ancient Hope for Our 21st Century World.* Shippensburg, PA: Destiny Image, 2004.

Munroe, Myles, and T.D. Jakes. *Myles Munroe Devotional & Journal: 365 Days to Realize Your Potential.* Shippensburg, PA: Destiny Image, 2007.

Pfau, Wade. "How Long Can Retirees Expect To Live Once They Hit 65?" *Forbes*, August 25, 2016. https://www.forbes.com/sites/wadepfau/2016/08/25/how-long-can-retirees-expect-to-live-once-they-hit-65.

Poterba, James M., Steven F. Venti, and David A. Wise. "Were They Prepared for Retirement? Financial Status at Advanced Ages in the HRS and AHEAD Cohorts." National Bureau of Economic Research, (February 2012). https://doi.org/10.3386/w17824.

Pugle, Michelle. "Can Stress Cause Death?" Psych Central, updated June 30, 2022. https://psychcentral.com/stress/is-stress-the-number-one-killer.

Rosanes, Mark. "These Are the World's 20 Largest Insurance Companies in 2022." Insurance *Business America*, September 23, 2022. https://www.insurancebusinessmag.com/us/guides/these-are-the-worlds-20-largest-insurance-companies-in-2022-421548.aspx.

Sammon, Alexander. "The Collapse of Long-Term Care Insurance." The American Prospect, October 20, 2020. https://prospect.org/familycare/the-collapse-of-long-term-care-insurance/.

Schell, Jennifer and Chip Stapleton, "Allianz Life," Annuity.org, updated November 17, 2023. https://www.annuity.org/annuities/providers/allianz-life/.

Smialek, Jeanna. "Inflation Cools to 5% in March, but It's a Long Road Back to Normal." *New York Times*, April 12, 2023. https://www.nytimes.com/2023/04/12/business/inflation-fed-rates.html.

Speers, Peggi, and Tia Walker. *The Inspired Caregiver: Finding Joy While Caring for Those You Love*. North Charleston, SC: CreateSpace Independent Publishing Platform, 2013.

"Study Shows Link between Testosterone and Women's Choice to Enter Finance Careers." *UChicago News*, August 25, 2009. https://news.uchicago.edu/story/study-shows-link-between-testosterone-and-womens-choice-enter-finance-careers.

"Top 7 Reasons Why 90% of US Millionaires Invest in Real Estate & Why You Should Follow the Lead." Red Oak Development Group, August 3, 2022. https://redoakvc.com/top-7-reasons-why-90-of-us-millionaires-invest-in-real-estate-why-you-should-follow-the-lead.

United States National War Labor Board. 1944. *Application of the "Little Steel" Formula.* Washington, DC: Division of Public Information.

"United States Reserve Requirement Ratio." CEIC, July 10, 2020. https://www.ceicdata.com/en/indicator/united-states/reserve-requirement-ratio.

"What Are the Marriage Requirements to Receive Social Security Spouse's Benefits? FAQ|SSA," Social Security Administration, last modified October 7, 2022. https://faq.ssa.gov/en-us/Topic/article/KA-01999.

"Why Insurers Differ from Banks." Insurance Europe, October 2014. https://www.insuranceeurope.eu/publications/488/why-insurers-differ-from-banks/.

"World's Top Asset Management Firms." ADV Ratings, updated June 30, 2023. https://www.advratings.com/top-asset-management-firms.

"WWEIA Data Tables: USDA ARS," Accessed September 12, 2023. https://www.ars.usda.gov/northeast-area/beltsville-md-bhnrc/beltsville-human-nutrition-research-center/food-surveys-research-group/docs/wweia-data-tables/.

Zuckerman, Peter, and Amanda Padoan. *Buried in the Sky: The Extraordinary Story of the Sherpa Climbers on K2's Deadliest Day.* New York: W.W. Norton, 2012.

ABOUT THE AUTHOR

ANDREW WINNETT is the founder of Retirement Renegade (formerly Legacy Builders Wealth Management). He serves clients across the country, helping them grow and protecting their retirement savings so they never lose a penny due to market volatility. Andrew is the host of the "Retirement Renegade Radio" show heard across the country and has been featured in numerous national publications. He is on NBC and CBS every weekend (watch these appearances and more at RetirementRenegade.com). He has produced two Hollywood-rated, retirement-focused movies called "The Baby Boomer Dilemma" and "The Retirement Deception." He has written four books: *Retire Without Fear* (formerly *The Joseph Strategy*), *Crash Proof Wealth*, *Her Safe Retirement*, and *Escape to Tennessee*. Outside of work, you'll find Andrew investing time with his four kids and lovely wife, Jess, in their home in Franklin, Tennessee.

Made in the USA
Monee, IL
10 May 2025